JOY

FROM THE
UPPER ROOM

A Flexible Inductive Study of
John 13-17

by
Pam Gillaspie

Joy From the Upper Room

Copyright © 2024 by Pam Gillaspie
Published by Ignite Bible Ministries
www.pamgillaspie.com

ISBN 978-1-960938-22-0

JOY
FROM THE
UPPER ROOM
John 13-17

Dedicated to . . .

Krista Boerman Malley. . . a woman of joy in every circumstance. You fought the good fight, you finished the course, you kept the faith. Your life has been and will continue to be an example to so many!

Acknowledgements

My most sincere thanks to my fellow students at New Hope Christian Community Church and at Immanuel Church for piloting this material with me. I am grateful to walk with you and learn together. Thanks, too, to my dear husband for your constant encouragement to follow God's call on my life. Your support means the world to me!

JOY

FROM THE UPPER ROOM

There is nothing quite like your favorite pair of jeans. You can dress them up, you can dress them down. You can work in them, play in them, shop in them . . . live in them. They always feel right. It is my hope that the structure of this Bible study will fit you like those jeans; that it will work with your life right now, right where you are whether you're new to this whole Bible thing or whether you've been studying the Book for years!

How is this even possible? Smoke and mirrors, perhaps? The new mercilessly thrown in the deep end? The experienced given pompoms and the job of simply cheering others on? None of the above.

Sweeter than Chocolate!® flexible studies are designed with options that will allow you to go as deep each week as you desire. If you're just starting out and feeling a little overwhelmed, stick with the main text and don't think a second thought about the sidebar assignments. If you're looking for a challenge, then take the sidebar prompts and go ahead and dig all the way to China! As you move along through the study, think of the sidebars and "Digging Deeper" boxes as that 2% of lycra that you find in certain jeans . . . the wiggle-room that will help them fit just right.

Beginners may find that they want to start adding in some of the optional assignments as they go along. Experts may find that when three children are throwing up for three days straight, foregoing those assignments for the week is the way to live wisely.

Life has a way of ebbing and flowing and this study is designed to ebb and flow right along with it!

Enjoy!

Contents

Lesson One
Dark Days and Dirty Feet 1

Lesson Two
Abandoned? Never! . . .15

Lesson Three
True Peace 31

Lesson Four
Abide in My Love . . . 45

Lesson Five
Not of This World . . . 61

Lesson Six
An Unexpected Advantage! 73

Lesson Seven
From Grief to Joy! . . 89

Lesson Eight
Jesus Prays for You! 103

Resources 120

How to use this study

Sweeter than Chocolate!® studies meet you where you are and take you as far as you want to go.

1. WEEKLY STUDY: The main text guides you through the complete topic of study for the week.

2. FYI boxes: For Your Information boxes provide bite-sized material to shed additional light on the topic.

3. ONE STEP FURTHER and other sidebar boxes: Sidebar boxes give you the option to push yourself a little further. If you have extra time or are looking for an extra challenge, you can try one, all, or any number in between! These boxes give you the ultimate in flexibility.

4. DIGGING DEEPER boxes: If you're looking to go further, Digging Deeper sections will help you sharpen your skills as you continue to mine the truths of Scripture for yourself.

Dark Days and Dirty Feet

*"If I then, the Lord and the Teacher, washed your feet,
you also ought to wash one another's feet."*
—Jesus, John 13:14

Last words matter. When we know the end is near, we lean in, we listen more intently. Often we look back and remember. As you read this, you may be recalling the final words of a beloved book or fictional character. You may be thinking back to the last days of a loved one or your last hours in that person's presence. When someone we love leaves us—whether through death or another kind of departure—our natural response is sadness and a sense of loss. Jesus, however, specializes in turning our natural responses into supernatural ones!

In John 13–17, the Apostle John records for us the final days and words of Jesus before He goes to the cross. The days include tender moments with the disciples, examples of service, and acts of betrayal. Before leaving, Jesus equips His disciples to thrive in His absence as He prays for them and shows them the way to joy made full even in the midst of life's darkest days.

FYI:

If You're in a Class

Begin **Week One** together on your first day of class. This will be a great way to start getting to know one another and will help those who are newer to Bible study get their bearings. You won't finish, but when you sit down to do your class work during the week, you'll already have a jump on it! And how great will that feel?!

JOY
FROM THE
UPPER ROOM
John 13-17

LESSON ONE: **Dark Days and Dirty Feet**

CONSIDER the WAY YOU THINK

We all come to Bible study with different views and experiences. Before we get started, let's consider some of those together.

What has been your experience with the Bible? Are you a reader? Do you consider yourself a student of the Word or is everything about this new to you? (If it's all new, that is great!! We'll all be learning straight from God's Word together!)

What are your expectations as we set out on this journey together? Are you seeking to know God in a more general sense or looking for answers to specific questions? Explain. If you have specific questions, go ahead and write them down.

Do you have any apprehensions about this study? If so, what are they? Facing and naming the concerns often helps to disarm and diminish them.

Finally, are you approaching this study with the primary purpose of learning what Jesus says, obeying what Jesus says, or both? Again, explain.

FYI:

Start with Prayer

You've probably heard it before and if we study together in the future, you're sure to hear it again. Whenever you read or study God's Word, first pray and ask His Spirit to be your Guide.

As the psalmist prays to God in Psalm 119:102, "I have not turned aside from Your ordinances, for You Yourself have taught me."

GETTING THE BIG PICTURE

John structures his gospel account around seven major miracles that Jesus performs over the course of His ministry beginning with His turning water into wine at the wedding in Cana of Galilee in John 2 and culminating with His raising Lazarus from the dead in John 11, just two chapters prior to the passage we'll be diving into.

John tells his reader in John 20:30-31 that Jesus performed many signs in the presence of His disciples that he did not write down, but the ones he did were "written so that you may believe that Jesus is the Christ, the Son of God; and that believing you may have life in His name."

Just prior to our passage, John 12 recounts Jesus entering Jerusalem on a donkey's colt to shouts of "Hosanna! BLESSED IS HE WHO COMES IN THE NAME OF THE LORD, even the King of Israel" (John 12:13) as He and His disciples come to the holy city to celebrate Passover.

OBSERVE the TEXT of SCRIPTURE

READ John 13 and **MARK** every reference to *Jesus* (include *He, Him, His*).

John 13

1 *Now before the Feast of the Passover, Jesus knowing that His hour had come that He would depart out of this world to the Father, having loved His own who were in the world, He loved them to the end.*

2 *During supper, the devil having already put into the heart of Judas Iscariot, the son of Simon, to betray Him,*

3 *Jesus, knowing that the Father had given all things into His hands, and that He had come forth from God and was going back to God,*

4 *got up from supper, and laid aside His garments; and taking a towel, He girded Himself.*

5 *Then He poured water into the basin, and began to wash the disciples' feet and to wipe them with the towel with which He was girded.*

6 *So He came to Simon Peter. He said to Him, "Lord, do You wash my feet?"*

7 *Jesus answered and said to him, "What I do you do not realize now, but you will understand hereafter."*

8 *Peter said to Him, "Never shall You wash my feet!" Jesus answered him, "If I do not wash you, you have no part with Me."*

9 *Simon Peter said to Him, "Lord, then wash not only my feet, but also my hands and my head."*

10 *Jesus said to him, "He who has bathed needs only to wash his feet, but is completely clean; and you are clean, but not all of you."*

11 *For He knew the one who was betraying Him; for this reason He said, "Not all of you are clean."*

12 *So when He had washed their feet, and taken His garments and reclined at the table again, He said to them, "Do you know what I have done to you?*

13 *"You call Me Teacher and Lord; and you are right, for so I am.*

FYI:

Passover
To this day, Jewish people celebrate the feast of Passover which commemorates God's deliverance of His people from Egyptian slavery. At the first Passover which happened at the time of the tenth plague against the Egyptians, God commanded that each Israelite household sacrifice a perfect lamb and put some of its blood on the two doorposts and lintel of their homes so that their homes would be "passed over" when the LORD struck all of Egypt's firstborn.

JOY
FROM THE
UPPER ROOM
John 13-17

LESSON ONE: **Dark Days and Dirty Feet**

ONE STEP FURTHER:

Listen through . . .

When I'm planning to spend an extended time in a Scripture passage (as we will be doing with John 13–17), I find it helpful to take in the Word a variety of ways.

First, we'll read the text repeatedly and mark some words as we go. You may even find yourself beginning to memorize some of it without trying! Slowing down and reading carefully is critical to the inductive process and marking is so helpful.

Listening, though, is an often-overlooked option for taking in the Word that you may want to add to your repertoire. You can to do this by reading the text aloud, by listening to an audio Bible, or by reading along with an audio Bible.

By listening we can redeem time even when we can't sit down and study. It is just one more way to help you meditate and delight in God's Word.

14 "If I then, the Lord and the Teacher, washed your feet, you also ought to wash one another's feet.

15 "For I gave you an example that you also should do as I did to you.

16 "Truly, truly, I say to you, a slave is not greater than his master, nor is one who is sent greater than the one who sent him.

17 "If you know these things, you are blessed if you do them.

18 "I do not speak of all of you. I know the ones I have chosen; but it is that the Scripture may be fulfilled, 'HE WHO EATS MY BREAD HAS LIFTED UP HIS HEEL AGAINST ME.'

19 "From now on I am telling you before it comes to pass, so that when it does occur, you may believe that I am He.

20 "Truly, truly, I say to you, he who receives whomever I send receives Me; and he who receives Me receives Him who sent Me."

21 When Jesus had said this, He became troubled in spirit, and testified and said, "Truly, truly, I say to you, that one of you will betray Me."

22 The disciples began looking at one another, at a loss to know of which one He was speaking.

23 There was reclining on Jesus' bosom one of His disciples, whom Jesus loved.

24 So Simon Peter gestured to him, and said to him, "Tell us who it is of whom He is speaking."

25 He, leaning back thus on Jesus' bosom, said to Him, "Lord, who is it?"

26 Jesus then answered, "That is the one for whom I shall dip the morsel and give it to him." So when He had dipped the morsel, He took and gave it to Judas, the son of Simon Iscariot.

27 After the morsel, Satan then entered into him. Therefore Jesus said to him, "What you do, do quickly."

28 Now no one of those reclining at the table knew for what purpose He had said this to him.

29 For some were supposing, because Judas had the money box, that Jesus was saying to him, "Buy the things we have need of for the feast"; or else, that he should give something to the poor.

30 So after receiving the morsel he went out immediately; and it was night.

31 Therefore when he had gone out, Jesus said, "Now is the Son of Man glorified, and God is glorified in Him;

32 if God is glorified in Him, God will also glorify Him in Himself, and will glorify Him immediately.

33 "Little children, I am with you a little while longer. You will seek Me; and as I said to the Jews, now I also say to you, 'Where I am going, you cannot come.'

34 "A new commandment I give to you, that you love one another, even as I have loved you, that you also love one another.

35 "By this all men will know that you are My disciples, if you have love for one another."

36 *Simon Peter said to Him, "Lord, where are You going?" Jesus answered, "Where I go, you cannot follow Me now; but you will follow later."*

37 *Peter said to Him, "Lord, why can I not follow You right now? I will lay down my life for You."*

38 *Jesus answered, "Will you lay down your life for Me? Truly, truly, I say to you, a rooster will not crow until you deny Me three times."*

DISCUSS with your GROUP or PONDER on your own . . .
WHO, WHAT, WHEN, WHERE, WHY, and HOW?

We will be going back and looking at this chapter section by section, so feel free to keep your answers brief for the following questions.

Briefly describe the setting. When and where does John 13 take place?

Who is the main character? Briefly describe what He is doing.

Now, looking at every place you marked references to Jesus, list what you learned about Him from this chapter.

Who else is mentioned? What are they up to?

NOTES

INDUCTIVE STUDY:

What is Inductive study?
When we study the Bible inductively, we simply use the Bible as our primary source to study the Bible. While this sounds beyond obvious, much of what people term "Bible study" today is more of a compilation of others' opinions about the Bible rather than biblical truth direct from the source.

In inductive study we let God speak for Himself through His Word. One of the ways we do this is by directing questions to the text. Not sure what to ask? Simply start with the 5Ws and H—*Who? What? When? Where? Why?* and *How?*

As we move through the study, you'll catch on to this process, and before you know it you'll be anticipating questions I ask . . . yourself!

In all truth, inductive Bible study teachers who teach well eventually teach themselves out of a job as their students learn and begin to teach others . . . who teach others . . . who teach others.

JOY
FROM THE
UPPER ROOM
John 13-17

Digging Deeper

The Whole Story

If you have time this week, start immersing yourself in the whole Gospel of John so you'll have greater context for the chapters that we are studying together. As you do this, simply read or listen chapter by chapter and write down a #hashtag or main idea from each chapter as you go. We'll start this week by reading the chapters leading up to the section that we're studying. Don't stress out over "getting the right answer." Just record the main idea, scene, or character you notice as you're reading or listening.

This is an exercise in paying attention to context and getting an overview. There will be time for plenty of details, but now is not that time!

John 1 —

John 2 —

John 3 —

John 4 —

John 5 —

John 6 —

John 7 —

John 8 —

John 9 —

John 10 —

John 11 —

John 12 —

Briefly summarize the content of John 1–12.

INDUCTIVE STUDY:

Letting the Text Speak

As we study together, it is my prayer that to the best of our ability we will drop our presuppositions and allow God's Word to speak for itself. There's so much freedom in this, isn't there? You don't have to come up with clever ideas and remotely possible "what ifs." You simply pay attention and learn from what God has clearly revealed.

When we do this, it's called *exegesis*. Exegesis literally means "to lead out." When we start with subjective presuppositions, we fall into the trap of *eisegesis* (literally "to lead into")—taking the text of Scripture and tailoring it to our agendas. Eisegesis molds Scripture to fit people; the Word accurately handled calls people to submit to the plumb line of Scripture. My goal for this class is that we handle accurately the Word of truth and have God speak to us and change *us* through it.

LOOKING CLOSER . . .

Now that we have a good overview of John 13, let's go back and look at it more closely section by section.

OBSERVE the TEXT of SCRIPTURE

READ John 13:1-4 and **MARK** the word *knowing*.

John 13:1-4

1 *Now before the Feast of the Passover, Jesus knowing that His hour had come that He would depart out of this world to the Father, having loved His own who were in the world, He loved them to the end.*

2 *During supper, the devil having already put into the heart of Judas Iscariot, the son of Simon, to betray Him,*

3 *Jesus, knowing that the Father had given all things into His hands, and that He had come forth from God and was going back to God,*

4 *got up from supper, and laid aside His garments; and taking a towel, He girded Himself.*

DISCUSS with your GROUP or PONDER on your own . . .

According to verses 1 and 3, what did Jesus know?

How did this knowledge affect what He did?

Does your knowledge of the Word of God affect what you do? Why/why not? Explain.

"His Hour Had Come"

If you have time this week, explore the phrase "His hour had come." You'll want to search on the Greek word for "hour" *(hora)* to find similar phrases and then go from there. If you're not sure where to start, try Blue Letter Bible (blueletterbible.com).

See if you can find out how John uses "hour" generally in his writings, then how he uses it here in 13:1.

What does "hour had come" mean?

ONE STEP FURTHER:

JOY
FROM THE
UPPER ROOM
John 13-17

LESSON ONE: **Dark Days and Dirty Feet**

What do Jesus' actions demonstrate?

Finally, what did you learn about God the Father in these verses?

OBSERVE the TEXT of SCRIPTURE

READ John 13:5-20. **MARK** every reference to *Peter* and every occurrence of the word *wash*.

John 13:5-20

5 *Then He poured water into the basin, and began to wash the disciples' feet and to wipe them with the towel with which He was girded.*

6 *So He came to Simon Peter. He said to Him, "Lord, do You wash my feet?"*

7 *Jesus answered and said to him, "What I do you do not realize now, but you will understand hereafter."*

8 *Peter said to Him, "Never shall You wash my feet!" Jesus answered him, "If I do not wash you, you have no part with Me."*

9 *Simon Peter said to Him, "Lord, then wash not only my feet, but also my hands and my head."*

10 *Jesus said to him, "He who has bathed needs only to wash his feet, but is completely clean; and you are clean, but not all of you."*

11 *For He knew the one who was betraying Him; for this reason He said, "Not all of you are clean."*

12 *So when He had washed their feet, and taken His garments and reclined at the table again, He said to them, "Do you know what I have done to you?*

13 *"You call Me Teacher and Lord; and you are right, for so I am.*

14 *"If I then, the Lord and the Teacher, washed your feet, you also ought to wash one another's feet.*

15 *"For I gave you an example that you also should do as I did to you.*

16 *"Truly, truly, I say to you, a slave is not greater than his master, nor is one who is sent greater than the one who sent him.*

17 *"If you know these things, you are blessed if you do them.*

18 *"I do not speak of all of you. I know the ones I have chosen; but it is that the Scripture may be fulfilled, 'HE WHO EATS MY BREAD HAS LIFTED UP HIS HEEL AGAINST ME.'*

19 *"From now on I am telling you before it comes to pass, so that when it does occur, you may believe that I am He.*

20 *"Truly, truly, I say to you, he who receives whomever I send receives Me; and he who receives Me receives Him who sent Me."*

DISCUSS with your GROUP or PONDER on your own . . .

What does Jesus do according to verses 5-17?

What happens when He comes to Simon Peter? How does Peter respond?

What does Jesus tell Peter that causes him to relent? Do people today have the same objection as Peter? If so, in what way(s)?

Do you ever push back against God's way of doing things preferring to try to clean yourself up in your own way? How and why? Can any of us clean ourselves up enough for Jesus? Explain.

What does Jesus explain to Peter? Who does He say is clean and why?

ONE STEP FURTHER:

Old Testament Fulfillment
If you have some extra time this week, find out where the quotation "HE WHO EATS MY BREAD HAS LIFTED UP HIS HEEL AGAINST ME" comes from. Who do you think David had in mind in his day and who does Jesus apply it to and why? Record what you discover below.

ONE STEP FURTHER:

Word Study: Clean
Take a couple of minutes to check your concordance for the word translated "clean" in John 13:10-11. See if you can identify the Greek word and find where else it is going to appear in John! When you find it, write it below. It will become important as we work through a difficult passage coming up in the next few weeks. One. Step. At. A. Time. Right?

JOY
FROM THE
UPPER ROOM
John 13-17

LESSON ONE: **Dark Days and Dirty Feet**

What lesson does Jesus want His disciples to learn from His example?

If you feel overwhelmed

I should probably say "When you feel overwhelmed." From time to time, life picks up speed and we discover one too many plates spinning.

On days or weeks like this, you may be tempted to set aside your time in the Word. I urge you to make a different decision. Instead of stopping, shift gears temporarily. Take a week, focus only on the Scripture, and leave the blanks, well, blank . . . . You can even use an audio Bible to help you redeem the time.

Whatever you do, don't stop because you feel a little busy. Adjust and stay in the Word.

How have others "washed your feet"? What effect did that have on you in the moment? How did it affect you long-term?

How can you "wash the feet" of those around you? What will it cost you in money? Time? Status?

How does Jesus' teaching about service compare with what the world teaches? Explain.

What does Jesus want His disciples (then and now!) to know and understand? What should this knowledge lead to?

What does Jesus prophesy about starting in verse 18? Why does He tell this to His disciples?

FROM THE
UPPER ROOM
John 13-17

10

OBSERVE the TEXT of SCRIPTURE

READ John 13:21-30 and **MARK** references to each of the people mentioned.

John 13:21-30

21 *When Jesus had said this, He became troubled in spirit, and testified and said, "Truly, truly, I say to you, that one of you will betray Me."*

22 *The disciples began looking at one another, at a loss to know of which one He was speaking.*

23 *There was reclining on Jesus' bosom one of His disciples, whom Jesus loved.*

24 *So Simon Peter gestured to him, and said to him, "Tell us who it is of whom He is speaking."*

25 *He, leaning back thus on Jesus' bosom, said to Him, "Lord, who is it?"*

26 *Jesus then answered, "That is the one for whom I shall dip the morsel and give it to him." So when He had dipped the morsel, He took and gave it to Judas, the son of Simon Iscariot.*

27 *After the morsel, Satan then entered into him. Therefore Jesus said to him, "What you do, do quickly."*

28 *Now no one of those reclining at the table knew for what purpose He had said this to him.*

29 *For some were supposing, because Judas had the money box, that Jesus was saying to him, "Buy the things we have need of for the feast"; or else, that he should give something to the poor.*

30 *So after receiving the morsel he went out immediately; and it was night.*

DISCUSS with your GROUP or PONDER on your own . . .

While we read that the disciples as a group are with Jesus, which ones are named (or described) specifically and what does each do?

What causes Jesus to become "troubled in spirit" in verse 21?

ONE STEP FURTHER:

"Troubled in Spirit"

Take some time this week to examine and consider how the phrase "troubled in spirit" is used with regard to Jesus in the book of John. As you look at these verses—being sure to read as much context as needed—ask: *Why is Jesus troubled?*

Please don't miss this one, there will be a follow-up soon and that will make it SO worthwhile!!

John 11:33

John 12:27

John 13:21

JOY
FROM THE
UPPER ROOM
John 13-17

LESSON ONE: **Dark Days and Dirty Feet**

How do the disciples respond when they hear that one of them will betray Jesus?

According to verse 26, which of the disciples finds out who the betrayer will be? How does Jesus identify the betrayer and what does He say to him?

Do the disciples follow what is going on? Explain.

How did Jesus' audience change according to John 13:30? Why do you think this matters?

OBSERVE the TEXT of SCRIPTURE

READ John 13:31-38 and **MARK** distinctively every occurrence to *glorify/glorified* and every reference to *love*.

John 13:31-38

31 Therefore when he had gone out, Jesus said, "Now is the Son of Man glorified, and God is glorified in Him;

32 if God is glorified in Him, God will also glorify Him in Himself, and will glorify Him immediately.

33 "Little children, I am with you a little while longer. You will seek Me; and as I said to the Jews, now I also say to you, 'Where I am going, you cannot come.'

34 *"A new commandment I give to you, that you love one another, even as I have loved you, that you also love one another.*

35 *"By this all men will know that you are My disciples, if you have love for one another."*

36 *Simon Peter said to Him, "Lord, where are You going?" Jesus answered, "Where I go, you cannot follow Me now; but you will follow later."*

37 *Peter said to Him, "Lord, why can I not follow You right now? I will lay down my life for You."*

38 *Jesus answered, "Will you lay down your life for Me? Truly, truly, I say to you, a rooster will not crow until you deny Me three times."*

DISCUSS with your GROUP or PONDER on your own . . .

Why do you think verse 31 opens with "Therefore"? What does it refer back to?

You marked the words *glorify/glorified*. Now, list what Jesus said about this. (Don't fret if it seems a bit unclear. We're going to see more of this verb and its corresponding noun *glory* and explore them further in coming weeks.)

At this point, what do you think Jesus' being glorified will involve? Explain.

In verses 33 and 34, Jesus tells the disciples one thing they *can't do* and then gives them a new commandment *to do*. What are these?

INDUCTIVE STUDY:

What's it there for?

It's corny, but memorable. Whenever you see the word "therefore" in the text of Scripture (or any other written material for that matter!), you want to ask, "What is the *therefore* there for?"

"Therefores" are constant reminders to us to pay attention to context, specifically to what has already been said.

LESSON ONE: **Dark Days and Dirty Feet**

Which of the two statements does Peter latch onto and what does he want to know? What does he say he will do for Jesus?

Briefly list what Jesus tells the disciples about loving one another. How are they to do it? Why are they do it? What will it show about them?

How are you doing at loving others? Does the way you treat other believers display to the world that you belong to Jesus . . . or does it say something else? Are there any changes you need to make today based on what you've been learning in the Word this week? If so, jot down your first step in obeying and what happens next.

@THE END OF THE DAY . . .

As you finish off your time of study today, spend some time praying and looking back over the notes you've taken and the verses of John 13. After you've reviewed, respond to these prompts and call it a day:

Summarize John 13 as succinctly as you can. Aim for one or two sentences.

Give John 13 a title or, if you prefer, a #hashtag.

#

Write down your primary application from this chapter. What will you do this week as a result of what you know from Jesus' teaching in John 13?

Abandoned? Never!

*"Do not let your heart be troubled; believe in God,
believe also in Me."*
—Jesus, John 14:1

At the end of John 13 and the beginning of John 14, we feel tensions rising. Jesus is leaving—but where is He going? What will happen to the disciples when He is gone? As troubling thoughts threaten, Jesus tells His disciples "believe in God, believe also in Me."

His words seem simple, powerful, and even obvious, but day-by-day, minute-by-minute, and meme-by-meme our world drips a contrary "believe" message. Almighty Pinterest commands us: "Believe in yourself!"

Independence may be the American way, but Jesus clearly states that it is not God's way. Jesus will go away, but He will not abandon His disciples! He will not leave them alone.

Let's go to the text as we begin John 14!

ONE STEP FURTHER:

Listening Reminder

Just a reminder that listening to the text is one way to spend more time becoming familiar with it. Even if you have plenty of time to sit down and read, having the chapters playing in the background as you go about household chores or driving may even help you memorize segments of it.

LESSON TWO: **Abandoned? Never!**

REMEMBERING

Briefly summarize John 13 answering the basic *Who? What? When? Where? Why?* and *How?* questions as applicable.

ONE STEP FURTHER:

Self-Assessment

Before you begin this week's assignment in earnest, take some time to assess what you've been applying from John 13.

What I learned:

What I did:

If you knew what to do and didn't act, why was that?

What I discovered through obedience (if applicable):

How others responded to my behavior:

What was the biggest truth you *learned* in your study last week? What was the most significant truth you *have begun to apply*?

OVERVIEW JOHN 14

John 14 opens with Jesus speaking.

OBSERVE the TEXT of SCRIPTURE

READ John 14 and **MARK** all references to *Jesus*. (Remember to mark *I, My, You*, etc. when these words refer to Jesus.)

John 14

1 "Do not let your heart be troubled; believe in God, believe also in Me.

2 "In My Father's house are many dwelling places; if it were not so, I would have told you; for I go to prepare a place for you.

3 "If I go and prepare a place for you, I will come again and receive you to Myself, that where I am, there you may be also.

4 "And you know the way where I am going."

5 Thomas said to Him, "Lord, we do not know where You are going, how do we know the way?"

6 Jesus said to him, "I am the way, and the truth, and the life; no one comes to the Father but through Me.

7 "If you had known Me, you would have known My Father also; from now on you know Him, and have seen Him."

8 Philip said to Him, "Lord, show us the Father, and it is enough for us."

9 Jesus said to him, "Have I been so long with you, and yet you have not come to know Me, Philip? He who has seen Me has seen the Father; how can you say, 'Show us the Father'?

10 *"Do you not believe that I am in the Father, and the Father is in Me? The words that I say to you I do not speak on My own initiative, but the Father abiding in Me does His works.*

11 *"Believe Me that I am in the Father and the Father is in Me; otherwise believe because of the works themselves.*

12 *"Truly, truly, I say to you, he who believes in Me, the works that I do, he will do also; and greater works than these he will do; because I go to the Father.*

13 *"Whatever you ask in My name, that will I do, so that the Father may be glorified in the Son.*

14 *"If you ask Me anything in My name, I will do it.*

15 *"If you love Me, you will keep My commandments.*

16 *"I will ask the Father, and He will give you another Helper, that He may be with you forever;*

17 that is *the Spirit of truth, whom the world cannot receive, because it does not see Him or know Him, but you know Him because He abides with you and will be in you.*

18 *"I will not leave you as orphans; I will come to you.*

19 *"After a little while the world will no longer see Me, but you will see Me; because I live, you will live also.*

20 *"In that day you will know that I am in My Father, and you in Me, and I in you.*

21 *"He who has My commandments and keeps them is the one who loves Me; and he who loves Me will be loved by My Father, and I will love him and will disclose Myself to him."*

22 *Judas (not Iscariot) said to Him, "Lord, what then has happened that You are going to disclose Yourself to us and not to the world?"*

23 *Jesus answered and said to him, "If anyone loves Me, he will keep My word; and My Father will love him, and We will come to him and make Our abode with him.*

24 *"He who does not love Me does not keep My words; and the word which you hear is not Mine, but the Father's who sent Me.*

25 *"These things I have spoken to you while abiding with you.*

26 *"But the Helper, the Holy Spirit, whom the Father will send in My name, He will teach you all things, and bring to your remembrance all that I said to you.*

27 *"Peace I leave with you; My peace I give to you; not as the world gives do I give to you. Do not let your heart be troubled, nor let it be fearful.*

28 *"You heard that I said to you, 'I go away, and I will come to you.' If you loved Me, you would have rejoiced because I go to the Father, for the Father is greater than I.*

29 *"Now I have told you before it happens, so that when it happens, you may believe.*

30 *"I will not speak much more with you, for the ruler of the world is coming, and he has nothing in Me;*

31 *but so that the world may know that I love the Father, I do exactly as the Father commanded Me. Get up, let us go from here."*

INDUCTIVE STUDY:

People are Key

A common concern I often hear among beginning inductive Bible study students is this: *"I have such a hard time identifying key words!"* Now this is not a huge deal when you're in a study and someone tells you what to mark, right? But the hope is that you will take the tools you're learning here and use them when you open the Word on your own! When no one is telling you what to mark, the idea of marking can be a bit daunting.

Sometimes identifying key words is easy. Think how "faith" almost leaps off the page when you read Hebrews 11. Other times, though, key words take time and attention to uncover.

So what's a person to do? First, realize that key words by definition are not wildly elusive. You won't be able to understand the text without them—so relax and take a breath. Second, go for the low-hanging fruit. After marking references to God (God, the Father, Jesus, the Spirit), mark references to people mentioned in the text like the author, the recipients of his writing, and others.

By the time you're done marking all the references to God and to the people mentioned you will have read the text enough times to start noticing other words that are repeating, too!

Remember, one of the biggest keys to good study is simply:

S...L...O...W...I...N...G D...O...W...N!

JOY
FROM THE
UPPER ROOM
John 13-17

LESSON TWO: **Abandoned? Never!**

DISCUSS with your GROUP or PONDER on your own . . .

By way of review, where is Jesus and who is He talking to? How do these respectively compare with the *where* and *who* of John 13?

Summarize the main points of the conversation.

Did you notice any key, repeating words? If so, jot them down. If not, don't worry—you'll discover them as we continue to study.

Looking back at where you marked references to Jesus, list the most significant truths John 14 tells us about Him.

LOOKING CLOSER . . .

As we slow down to look more closely at John 14, we need to dial it back and review the last few verses of John 13 as they tie in closely with the beginning of this chapter.

REVIEWING JOHN 13:33-38

As you'll recall from our study last week, at the end of John 13 Jesus told His disciples to "love one another" even as He had loved them. He also said that He would be with them a little while longer. However, rather than focus on the command in

front of them, the disciples are overcome by the question: *"Where is Jesus going?!"* Let's look again at John 13:33-38 and consider what Jesus says and what the disciples ask Him.

OBSERVE the TEXT of SCRIPTURE

READ John 13:33-38 and **MARK** every occurrence of *where*. Then, **UNDERLINE** the questions Peter asks Jesus.

John 13:33-38

33 *"Little children, I am with you a little while longer. You will seek Me; and as I said to the Jews, now I also say to you, 'Where I am going, you cannot come.'*

34 *"A new commandment I give to you, that you love one another, even as I have loved you, that you also love one another.*

35 *"By this all men will know that you are My disciples, if you have love for one another."*

36 *Simon Peter said to Him, "Lord, where are You going?" Jesus answered, "Where I go, you cannot follow Me now; but you will follow later."*

37 *Peter said to Him, "Lord, why can I not follow You right now? I will lay down my life for You."*

38 *Jesus answered, "Will you lay down your life for Me? Truly, truly, I say to you, a rooster will not crow until you deny Me three times."*

DISCUSS with your GROUP or PONDER on your own . . .

What do we know about "where" Jesus is going just from these verses?

Where had Jesus twice said He was going in John 13:1-3?

What two questions does Peter ask Jesus?

FYI:

"Going back to . . ."
Now before the Feast of the Passover, Jesus knowing that His hour had come that He would depart out of this world to the Father, having loved His own who were in the world, He loved them to the end. During supper, the devil having already put into the heart of Judas Iscariot, the son of Simon, to betray Him, Jesus, knowing that the Father had given all things into His hands, and that He had come forth from God and was going back to God . . .

—John 13:1-3

LESSON TWO: **Abandoned? Never!**

While Jesus is talking about the disciples loving one another, what is Peter's main concern?

Have you ever experienced or feared abandonment? How did it affect your thinking in the moment or subsequently?

Have you ever felt abandoned by God? Why? If so, what scriptural truths do you bring to mind when you struggle with these feelings? (If you don't have any yet, you'll find them before this study is over!!!)

ONE STEP FURTHER:

More on "Troubled"

In John 11, 12, and 13 we see instances of Jesus being "troubled." Today, take some time to see and consider what He says to His disciples about having troubled hearts.

John 14:1

John 14:27

OBSERVE the TEXT of SCRIPTURE

READ John 14:1-7 and **MARK** in a consistent way any references to place or location (*house, place, where,* etc.). Also **MARK** occurrences of *know/known.*

John 14:1-7

1 *"Do not let your heart be troubled; believe in God, believe also in Me.*

2 *"In My Father's house are many dwelling places; if it were not so, I would have told you; for I go to prepare a place for you.*

3 *"If I go and prepare a place for you, I will come again and receive you to Myself, that where I am, there you may be also.*

4 *"And you know the way where I am going."*

5 *Thomas said to Him, "Lord, we do not know where You are going, how do we know the way?"*

6 *Jesus said to him, "I am the way, and the truth, and the life; no one comes to the Father but through Me.*

7 *"If you had known Me, you would have known My Father also; from now on you know Him, and have seen Him."*

DISCUSS with your GROUP or PONDER on your own . . .

What does Jesus tell His disciples *not to do* in verse 1?

What had Jesus been troubled about in John 13:21? What might the disciples be troubled about in coming days given what Jesus has been telling them?

Is there anything troubling your heart today? If so, write it down and keep it in mind as we continue.

What positive commands does Jesus give His disciples in verse 1?

What is involved in "believing in" Jesus, and what result does it bring? Let's take a look at a few cross-references from within the Gospel of John.

John 1:12

John 2:11

John 3:16-18

JOY
FROM THE
UPPER ROOM
John 13-17

LESSON TWO: **Abandoned? Never!**

John 6:40

John 11:25-27

John 12:44-46

Summarize what these verses teach about "believing in" Jesus.

What did you learn by marking references to place and location? Where does Jesus say He is going? What is He going to do there? How does this compare with John 13:1-3?

What hope does Jesus give the disciples in verse 3-4?

Why do you think Thomas is still confused after Jesus explains where He is going?

How does Jesus describe Himself in John 14:6? How does this answer Thomas's question?

ONE STEP FURTHER:

Word Studies: Way, Truth, Life

If you have some extra time this week, see if you can find the Greek words that are translated "way," "truth," and "life" in John 14:6. Once you've found them, see how else they are used in the Gospel of John and in the rest of the New Testament.

Way

Truth

Life

JOY
FROM THE
UPPER ROOM
John 13-17

How does the common cultural view that many roads lead to God compare with Jesus' statement? Why can Jesus make this statement?

How would you respond to the accusation that Christianity is a religion of exclusivity? (Word your response winsomely as though speaking to someone who disagrees with you. Think about whether you'd make a statement or ask a question in reply. Explain your thinking.)

SEEING the BIGGER PICTURE

Now, let's think for a moment about the bigger biblical narrative. Has there ever before been a place that God prepared for man where man would live in God's presence and in fellowship with Him? Let's go all the way back to the beginning for our answer!

OBSERVE the TEXT of SCRIPTURE

The history of mankind begins with human beings in relationship with and in the presence of God. I have so much more to say, but I need to stop so you can see for yourself! Let's take a look at what God tells us in Genesis 1–3.

READ Genesis 1–2 in your Bible or at the link in the margin.

DISCUSS with your GROUP or PONDER on your own . . .

What does God do in Genesis 1 and 2 before creating man? How does this compare with what Jesus says He is going to do in John 14:2-3?

FYI:

Another Resource
As you read Genesis 1–2 today, consider using www.biblehub.com as your text so you can explore this excellent online Bible study resource.

OBSERVE the TEXT of SCRIPTURE

READ Genesis 3 and **MARK** references to *God*.

Genesis 3

1 Now the serpent was more crafty than any beast of the field which the LORD God had made. And he said to the woman, "Indeed, has God said, 'You shall not eat from any tree of the garden'?"

2 The woman said to the serpent, "From the fruit of the trees of the garden we may eat;

3 but from the fruit of the tree which is in the middle of the garden, God has said, 'You shall not eat from it or touch it, or you will die.' "

4 The serpent said to the woman, "You surely will not die!

5 "For God knows that in the day you eat from it your eyes will be opened, and you will be like God, knowing good and evil."

6 When the woman saw that the tree was good for food, and that it was a delight to the eyes, and that the tree was desirable to make one wise, she took from its fruit and ate; and she gave also to her husband with her, and he ate.

7 Then the eyes of both of them were opened, and they knew that they were naked; and they sewed fig leaves together and made themselves loin coverings.

8 They heard the sound of the LORD God walking in the garden in the cool of the day, and the man and his wife hid themselves from the presence of the LORD God among the trees of the garden.

9 Then the LORD God called to the man, and said to him, "Where are you?"

10 He said, "I heard the sound of You in the garden, and I was afraid because I was naked; so I hid myself."

11 And He said, "Who told you that you were naked? Have you eaten from the tree of which I commanded you not to eat?"

12 The man said, "The woman whom You gave to be with me, she gave me from the tree, and I ate."

13 Then the LORD God said to the woman, "What is this you have done?" And the woman said, "The serpent deceived me, and I ate."

14 The LORD God said to the serpent, "Because you have done this, cursed are you more than all cattle, and more than every beast of the field; on your belly you will go, and dust you will eat all the days of your life;

15 and I will put enmity between you and the woman, and between your seed and her seed; he shall bruise you on the head, and you shall bruise him on the heel."

16 To the woman He said, "I will greatly multiply your pain in childbirth, in pain you will bring forth children; yet your desire will be for your husband, and he will rule over you."

17 Then to Adam He said, "Because you have listened to the voice of your wife, and have eaten from the tree about which I commanded you, saying, 'You shall not eat from it'; cursed is the ground because of you; in toil you will eat of it all the days of your life.

18 "Both thorns and thistles it shall grow for you; and you will eat the plants of the field;

19 by the sweat of your face you will eat bread, till you return to the ground, because from it you were taken; for you are dust, and to dust you shall return."

20 Now the man called his wife's name Eve, because she was the mother of all the living.

21 The LORD God made garments of skin for Adam and his wife, and clothed them.

22 Then the LORD God said, "Behold, the man has become like one of Us, knowing good and evil; and now, he might stretch out his hand, and take also from the tree of life, and eat, and live forever"—

23 therefore the LORD God sent him out from the garden of Eden, to cultivate the ground from which he was taken.

24 So He drove the man out; and at the east of the garden of Eden He stationed the cherubim and the flaming sword which turned every direction to guard the way to the tree of life.

DISCUSS with your GROUP or PONDER on your own . . .

Look at every place you marked "God" in the text. What key truths did you learn about His relationship with mankind?

What one negative command had God given to Adam?

What happened when Adam and Eve disobeyed God? What entered the world? How was their relationship with God affected?

ONE STEP FURTHER:

Your Turn!

If you have time this week, make a list of everything you learned about God in Genesis 3. You'll probably want to write small!

LESSON TWO: **Abandoned? Never!**

What happened to the place that God had prepared for them?

Although sin enters the world and death through sin, and although God banishes Adam and Eve from the place He had prepared for them and had been in fellowship with them, He does not leave them without hope.

In Genesis 3:15 we see the first glimpse of the gospel. Who is it addressed to? What does it prophesy?

While there is so much to learn from this chapter, we'll address just one more question before heading back to John.

Why did God banish Adam and Eve from the garden? What was He preventing?

Moving Back to John . . .

As we move back to John 14, note that I've included verse 7 again as it provides helpful context. Also note that the "yous" in verse 7 are plural.

OBSERVE the TEXT of SCRIPTURE

READ John 14:7-15 and **MARK** in a distinctive way the words *know/known* and the word *seen*.

John 14:7-15

7 *"If you had known Me, you would have known My Father also; from now on you know Him, and have seen Him."*

8 *Philip said to Him, "Lord, show us the Father, and it is enough for us."*

9 *Jesus said to him, "Have I been so long with you, and yet you have not come to know Me, Philip? He who has seen Me has seen the Father; how can you say, 'Show us the Father'?*

10 *"Do you not believe that I am in the Father, and the Father is in Me? The words that I say to you I do not speak on My own initiative, but the Father abiding in Me does His works.*

11 *"Believe Me that I am in the Father and the Father is in Me; otherwise believe because of the works themselves.*

12 *"Truly, truly, I say to you, he who believes in Me, the works that I do, he will do also; and greater works than these he will do; because I go to the Father.*

13 *"Whatever you ask in My name, that will I do, so that the Father may be glorified in the Son.*

14 *"If you ask Me anything in My name, I will do it.*

15 *"If you love Me, you will keep My commandments."*

DISCUSS with your GROUP or PONDER on your own . . .

Again, according to verse 7 what does Jesus tell the disciples they have already seen? Explain.

Compare what Jesus says in verse 7 with John 1:1-4 and 1:14-18. What do each of these texts teach about Jesus and His relationship with the Father?

John 1:1-4

John 1:14-18

Now, think this through. What has Philip been doing for the past three years? Who has physically been present alongside of him? And yet, what does Philip ask in verse 8?

Digging Deeper

That you might believe . . .

How much do we resemble Philip?

Before we throw Philip under the bus, let's take a step back and consider our times. It's not uncommon today for people to claim to be desperate for "a word from God" and yet never open their Bibles. Perhaps they even pray, "Lord, speak to me and it will be enough" while their Bibles remain closed.

Do we underestimate the blessing of the written Word of God and the indwelling of the Spirit as much as Philip underestimated the blessing of being in the presence of Christ? I'm just thinking . . .

Your thoughts?

John, under the inspiration of the Holy Spirit, wrote five of the twenty-seven New Testament books: the Gospel of John, three letters (1st, 2nd, and 3rd John), and Revelation. The Gospel of John and 1 John were each written with a purpose having to do specifically with belief. Record those purposes below.

John 20:30-31 —

1 John 5:13 —

If you feel like digging more this week, see what you can discover about how "believe" (Greek: *pisteuo*) and its noun form "faith" (Greek: *pistis*) are used in throughout the Bible starting with the Upper Room Discourse of John 13–17 and moving out contextually from there.

John 13–17

Gospel of John

Other Writings of John

New Testament

Old Testament

Do you think people today are ever as unaware of their spiritual blessings as Philip was? Are you? Explain.

How does Jesus respond to Philip? What has Philip been missing?

What does Jesus call Philip to do and why?

What does Jesus say about the works He has done and the works that His disciples will do?

Describe Jesus' relationship to the Father from this text. (This will be important to remember, especially as we head into John 15.)

How can people see the Father in the Son?

JOY
FROM THE
UPPER ROOM
John 13-17

LESSON TWO: **Abandoned? Never!**

How will people see the Son in you? Do you live with the front-of-mind realization that your life reflects on your heavenly Father? What kind of difference can that thinking make?

What does Jesus say about prayer in verses 13 and 14? How are we to ask? How will Jesus respond and why?

Finally (don't worry, we'll come back to this more next week!), how does Jesus describe the ones who love Him?

@THE END OF THE DAY . . .

Take some time to prayerfully review the pages of your study and identify key application points you'd like to focus on this week. Once you've done that, select one that you believe is most important to your walk with Christ, write it below, and ask God to align your life to that specific truth from His Word.

True Peace

"Peace I leave with you; My peace I give to you;
not as the world gives do I give to you.
Do not let your heart be troubled, nor let it be fearful."
—Jesus, John 14:27

Do you long for peace? How often do we think things like, "If only he would resign, everyone would get along" or "If they'd just fire her, then we'd have some peace around here"? Maybe it's "If that group of people would just stop rabble-rousing, the rest of us could get along" or "If only I had a little security in life, maybe I'd be able to sleep at night."

Human beings long for peace, but sin wars against it. Throughout the Bible we see the tension and struggle as God reconciles and restores people who were at war with Him back into a peaceful relationship first with Himself and then with one another.

The world is quick to promise a shadow peace, counterfeits rooted in money, status, relationships, health, and more, but each is fleeting. The peace of a fat account shrinks when Wall Street totters, the peace of good genes crumbles with the diagnosis of disease, the peace of the perfect friend or soul mate vanishes in the face of death or departure.

The Prince of Peace offers the only authentic goods around!

FYI:

Remember to Flex!

When life's a grind . . . remember to let your homework flex! Bend with pressure, don't break. Instead of allowing circumstances to overwhelm you and break your discipline, allow yourself to do a little less on exceptionally full days, but try to do something.

Football fans know that a "bend, don't break" defense willingly yields a few yards when it doesn't matter so it won't give up big yards when it does!

FYI:

Always Apply

Remember, we can't live what we don't know, but we can learn truth intellectually without living it. Just ask the Pharisees how that worked out for them . . .

ONE STEP FURTHER:

"Do Not Let Your Heart Be Troubled"

In John 11:33, 12:27, and 13:21 John records Jesus being "troubled in spirit" as He endures the death of Lazarus, faces the cross on our behalf, and watches Judas betray Him to that end.

The Greek *tarasso*—here translated "troubled"—means to be stirred up or agitated.

In John 14:1 and 27 Jesus has something better for us! He tells us that we are not to let our hearts be stirred up and troubled. We don't need to be troubled; He has dealt with the ultimate trouble on our behalf.

What does He tell us to do instead of being troubled? What has He given us so we don't have to be troubled? Jot down the answers from John 14:1 and John 14:27.

John 14:1

John 14:27

LESSON THREE: **True Peace**

REMEMBERING

Briefly summarize what you've learned so far from John 13 and the first half of John 14.

How are you doing at living what you are learning? What specific truth(s) have you been applying so far?

OVERVIEW JOHN 14

Because we'll be jumping into the second half of John 14 this week, let's go back and read the whole chapter again for context.

OBSERVE the TEXT of SCRIPTURE

READ John 14. Since we **MARKED** references to Jesus last week, let's **MARK** references to *the Father* and to *the Holy Spirit* (each in a distinctive way) this week. As you do this, remember to include any other words that refer to each of them, too.

John 14

1 *"Do not let your heart be troubled; believe in God, believe also in Me.*

2 *"In My Father's house are many dwelling places; if it were not so, I would have told you; for I go to prepare a place for you.*

3 *"If I go and prepare a place for you, I will come again and receive you to Myself, that where I am,* there *you may be also.*

4 *"And you know the way where I am going."*

5 *Thomas said to Him, "Lord, we do not know where You are going, how do we know the way?"*

6 *Jesus said to him, "I am the way, and the truth, and the life; no one comes to the Father but through Me.*

7 *"If you had known Me, you would have known My Father also; from now on you know Him, and have seen Him."*

8 *Philip said to Him, "Lord, show us the Father, and it is enough for us."*

9 *Jesus said to him, "Have I been so long with you, and yet you have not come to know Me, Philip? He who has seen Me has seen the Father; how can you say, 'Show us the Father'?*

10   *"Do you not believe that I am in the Father, and the Father is in Me? The words that I say to you I do not speak on My own initiative, but the Father abiding in Me does His works.*

11   *"Believe Me that I am in the Father and the Father is in Me; otherwise believe because of the works themselves.*

12   *"Truly, truly, I say to you, he who believes in Me, the works that I do, he will do also; and greater works than these he will do; because I go to the Father.*

13   *"Whatever you ask in My name, that will I do, so that the Father may be glorified in the Son.*

14   *"If you ask Me anything in My name, I will do it.*

15   *"If you love Me, you will keep My commandments.*

16   *"I will ask the Father, and He will give you another Helper, that He may be with you forever;*

17   *that is the Spirit of truth, whom the world cannot receive, because it does not see Him or know Him, but you know Him because He abides with you and will be in you.*

18   *"I will not leave you as orphans; I will come to you.*

19   *"After a little while the world will no longer see Me, but you will see Me; because I live, you will live also.*

20   *"In that day you will know that I am in My Father, and you in Me, and I in you.*

21   *"He who has My commandments and keeps them is the one who loves Me; and he who loves Me will be loved by My Father, and I will love him and will disclose Myself to him."*

22   *Judas (not Iscariot) said to Him, "Lord, what then has happened that You are going to disclose Yourself to us and not to the world?"*

23   *Jesus answered and said to him, "If anyone loves Me, he will keep My word; and My Father will love him, and We will come to him and make Our abode with him.*

24   *"He who does not love Me does not keep My words; and the word which you hear is not Mine, but the Father's who sent Me.*

25   *"These things I have spoken to you while abiding with you.*

26   *"But the Helper, the Holy Spirit, whom the Father will send in My name, He will teach you all things, and bring to your remembrance all that I said to you.*

27   *"Peace I leave with you; My peace I give to you; not as the world gives do I give to you. Do not let your heart be troubled, nor let it be fearful.*

28   *"You heard that I said to you, 'I go away, and I will come to you.' If you loved Me, you would have rejoiced because I go to the Father, for the Father is greater than I.*

29   *"Now I have told you before it happens, so that when it happens, you may believe.*

30   *"I will not speak much more with you, for the ruler of the world is coming, and he has nothing in Me;*

31   *but so that the world may know that I love the Father, I do exactly as the Father commanded Me. Get up, let us go from here."*

ONE STEP FURTHER:

A List about the Father

Take some time to list what you learned about the Father in John 14. If you're a detail person, knock yourself out! If you prefer to stay with the main points, that's okay, too. I'm praying you'll take at least a little time to look back at where you marked references to the Father and see how that can help in compiling a list of facts that you may otherwise overlook. Have at it in the space below.

JOY
FROM THE
UPPER ROOM
John 13-17

INDUCTIVE STUDY:

5Ws and H Prompts

Imagine this scenario. You're away from home and away from any Bible study workbooks. You have a Bible, a couple of pencils, and some time. Here's a simple way to remember how to start marking the text of Scripture when it's just you, your Bible, the Spirit, and a pencil. Just start with the 5Ws and H and let these serve as prompts.

Who? Mark references to God and any people you notice.

These will also be key words.

Whenever you have a key word, you can always list what you've learned about it.

What? Mark "what" the passage is about.

As you ask "What?" questions, you'll often discover key words.

Pay close attention to any words that repeat.

When? Circle (I do it in green) every reference to time.

This can refer to days, months, years.

It can also refer to time and sequence: *now, then, after,* etc.

Where? Double underline (I do this in green, too) every reference to geographical locations.

Why? Mark words and phrases like "because," "for this reason," "therefore," etc.

Terms of conclusion and causation will often answer "Why?" questions.

How? Pay attention to verbs, as they will often help answer "How?" questions.

JOY
FROM THE
UPPER ROOM
John 13-17

LESSON THREE: **True Peace**

DISCUSS with your GROUP or PONDER on your own . . .

What general observations did you have on John 14?

Did you notice any repeating key words? If so, write them down. If not, no worries! Move on to the next question. :)

What main topics does Jesus address in this chapter?

Where does the chapter begin? Who is there? What happens at the end?

LOOKING CLOSER . . .

In John 14:1-14 Jesus calls His disciples to belief even as He announces that He is going away to prepare a place for them. He assures them that because they have seen Him, they have seen the Father also.

OBSERVE the TEXT of SCRIPTURE

READ John 14:15-24 and **UNDERLINE PHRASES** that contain the following words: *love, keep,* and *commandment* or *word*. Also **MARK** in a distinctive way any form of the words *abide* and *love*.

John 14:15-24

15 *"If you love Me, you will keep My commandments.*

16 *"I will ask the Father, and He will give you another Helper, that He may be with you forever;*

17 that is *the Spirit of truth, whom the world cannot receive, because it does not see Him or know Him,* but *you know Him because He abides with you and will be in you.*

18 *"I will not leave you as orphans; I will come to you.*

19 *"After a little while the world will no longer see Me, but you* will *see Me; because I live, you will live also.*

20 *"In that day you will know that I am in My Father, and you in Me, and I in you.*

21 *"He who has My commandments and keeps them is the one who loves Me; and he who loves Me will be loved by My Father, and I will love him and will disclose Myself to him."*

22 *Judas (not Iscariot) said to Him, "Lord, what then has happened that You are going to disclose Yourself to us and not to the world?"*

23 *Jesus answered and said to him, "If anyone loves Me, he will keep My word; and My Father will love him, and We will come to him and make Our abode with him.*

24 *"He who does not love Me does not keep My words; and the word which you hear is not Mine, but the Father's who sent Me."*

DISCUSS with your GROUP or PONDER on your own . . .

Write down the phrases that you underlined.

What does Jesus say those who love Him will do?

What does this say to the person who claims the name Jesus but rejects His words and disobeys His commands?

ONE STEP FURTHER:

Another Helper
"Another" Helper? "Another" presup-poses the existence of more than one of something. So who is that? Take some time today and use your concordance to search on the word translated "Helper." You'll find that it only occurs in John and 1 John. The 1 John reference will probably help to clear things up! Find that and then record below what you discover.

LESSON THREE: **True Peace**

Has Jesus defined any specific commandments yet in this passage? (See John 13:34.)

What does Jesus say He will ask the Father for? (We'll see Him actually do this in John 17!)

From the text, list what we know about the Helper. What else is He called? How long will He be with the disciples? etc.

In verse 17, how does Jesus contrast the disciples and the world?

How is it that the disciples already know the Spirit of truth? (Reason through verses 16 and 17 as you answer.)

What will change in Jesus' relationship with His disciples after He leaves?

JOY
FROM THE
UPPER ROOM
John 13-17

According to verse 20, what will Jesus' disciples know "in that day"? What does this say about our relationship not only with Jesus but also with the Father?

How does this differ from what the world will experience?

Looking back at where you marked "love," write down everything you learned about it from this passage.

Based on these verses, is it possible to love Jesus and live any way you want to? Explain.

What does Jesus say about "abiding" in verses 17 and 23?

LESSON THREE: **True Peace**

Digging Deeper

God's Love and Our Love

Paul's 1 Corinthians 13 may be known as the "Love" chapter, but John also writes extensively on love and outpaces the other gospel writers—Matthew, Mark, and Luke—in talking about this important topic.

If you have time this week, examine what John writes about "love" throughout his gospel account, paying particular attention to what he says in our passage at hand (John 13–17). Then read 1 John and do the same!

What John says about love in the Gospel of John:

What John says about love in 1 John:

What I've learned about love that I can apply in my life today:

OBSERVE the TEXT of SCRIPTURE

READ John 14:25-31 and **MARK** references to *peace*.

John 14:25-31

25 *"These things I have spoken to you while abiding with you.*

26 *"But the Helper, the Holy Spirit, whom the Father will send in My name, He will teach you all things, and bring to your remembrance all that I said to you.*

27 *"Peace I leave with you; My peace I give to you; not as the world gives do I give to you. Do not let your heart be troubled, nor let it be fearful.*

28 *"You heard that I said to you, 'I go away, and I will come to you.' If you loved Me, you would have rejoiced because I go to the Father, for the Father is greater than I.*

29 *"Now I have told you before it happens, so that when it happens, you may believe.*

30 *"I will not speak much more with you, for the ruler of the world is coming, and he has nothing in Me;*

31 *but so that the world may know that I love the Father, I do exactly as the Father commanded Me. Get up, let us go from here."*

DISCUSS with your GROUP or PONDER on your own . . .

Jesus makes the first of several "these things I have spoken" statements in verse 25. What does He say about what He has spoken?

How has Jesus been abiding with them? What has it involved?

Who are mentioned in verse 26? What will each do? How will this help the disciples?

JOY
FROM THE
UPPER ROOM
John 13-17

ONE STEP FURTHER:

Other Translations

If you have some extra time this week, you may want to read John 13–17 in a couple of other versions. If you do, write down the versions you use and record some of the variations you observe. Remember, the NASB, the ESV, and the NKJV provide solid word-for-word translations from the original languages. Other versions we sometimes deem "easier" to read are so because the translators have done interpretive work for us that may or may not be correct. Easier may seem helpful but easy doesn't necessarily equal accurate. You'll understand what translators think texts mean but what they actually mean may be obscured.

LESSON THREE: **True Peace**

What else does Jesus promise to give His disciples in verse 27? Because of this, how will they be able to live?

Take a minute to put yourself in the disciples' shoes. If Jesus told you He was leaving, what fears do you think you would have?

On another note, what fears are you dealing with today?

In what ways does the world offer peace to combat people's fears? Do you ever seek peace the world's way? How has that worked for you? How have you observed it working for others?

How does Jesus' peace differ? Here are just a few verses to give us more insight into the peace He gives. There are many, many more, but these will give us a start:

Romans 5:1

Romans 8:6

Romans 14:17

Romans 15:33

2 Corinthians 13:11

Galatians 5:22

Ephesians 2:14-18

Philippians 4:6-9

Colossians 1:20

2 Thessalonians 3:16

James 3:17

Briefly summarize what you learned from the cross-references about the peace Jesus gives.

Why does Jesus tell the disciples they should rejoice? Do you think it has anything to do with John 14:23? Explain.

ONE STEP FURTHER:

Peace in the Old Testament
Want to dig more into peace? Take some time looking into the Old Testament word for peace this week. Start by finding the Hebrew word for peace (you'll recognize it when you see it!) and trace the concept through the Old Testament. Record your findings below.

What has Jesus told the disciples in advance so far in John 13 and 14? How will knowing in advance benefit them?

ONE STEP FURTHER:

Who Is "The Ruler of This World" and Why?

If you have some extra time this week, see what you can find out about "the ruler of this world." Who is he? What kind of power does he have? Where does he get his authority/power?

While we can search on a word that will bring us to all relevant cross-references we need, this one is a little more difficult.

First, then, think through how you can go about finding references you'll need. A concordance is a good start, but what other tools can help you?

Spend some time figuring out how to tackle this question, then get at it! If you have a hard time, don't worry and move on. Revisit the search another day.

Remember, this is not just about filling in answers, I want you to be equipped to study God's Word for yourselves. Part of this involves knowing how to dig and knowing what tools to use when!

Why does Jesus say He will "not speak much more" with the disciples?

Who do you think Jesus is referring to when He refers to "the ruler of this world"? Explain your answer from Scripture.

According to verse 31, what example does Jesus give with reference to His relationship with the Father? Why did He obey the Father? Where should our obedience be rooted?

How do you compare? When you obey God, why do you obey Him?

Finally, what change of venue happens at the end of John 14? Again, where are Jesus and His disciples?

Digging Deeper

Let's Memorize

God has used His Word to change my life and conform me to the image of His Son. You all know that I'm not all the way there yet but He has brought me so far from what I was and from what I would have been apart from Him. Much of the work He has done in me has been through memorizing Scripture. As we're studying John 13–17 together, I'm doing my best to memorize as much of it as possible as we go along primarily by listening to it over and over again. I'll give you some specific tools and tips in upcoming lessons, but for now I would love for you to pick out a verse or short passage from John 13 and one from John 14 to commit to memory or at least meditate on thoroughly! What do you think? Are you with me?! If so—and I trust you are!—write them below.

John 13

John 14

Didn't give you too much space to overwhelm you, did I?

@THE END OF THE DAY . . .

As you finish off your study today, spend some time praying and looking back over John 14. Then, respond to these prompts and call it day:

Summarize John 14 as succinctly as you can. Aim for one or two sentences.

Give John 14 a #hashtag.

#

Write down your most significant application from John 14. What will you do this week as a result of what you've learned? How can you obey *today*?

JOY
FROM THE
UPPER ROOM
John 13-17

LESSON THREE: **True Peace**

Abide in My Love

"My Father is glorified by this, that you bear much fruit,
and so prove to be My disciples."
—Jesus, John 15:8

As I write this lesson, it's been quite a month. I knew it going in. I thought about it, I prayed about it, and I realized that the only way I'd make it through would be by the grace of God. Maybe you're like me—when I think my time is "my own" and my account is full of hours and minutes, I'm not as aware of my need for God, but when I'm whelmed with life I realize more acutely what a weak and dependent creature I am. If He doesn't power the ship, my boat is going nowhere fast! If He doesn't grow the fruit, my branch will wither. The only way forward in the Christian life is abiding in the true Vine!

FYI:

Mid-Season!

Can you believe it? When we finish this lesson, we'll be halfway through our course of study. You're doing great! Keep it up and let's keep encouraging one another as we continue to move forward!

Let us hold fast the confession of our hope without wavering, for He who promised is faithful; and let us consider how to stimulate one another to love and good deeds, not forsaking our own assembling together, as is the habit of some, but encouraging one another; and all the more as you see the day drawing near.

—Hebrews 10:23-25

LESSON FOUR: **Abide in My Love**

REMEMBERING

Take a few minutes to summarize what you learned last week.

What truth(s) have you been most actively applying?

Have you been committing any verses to memory? If so, take a moment and write what you've memorized below.

OVERVIEW JOHN 15

We'll be spending the next couple of weeks on John 15 but let's go ahead and start overviewing the whole chapter today.

OBSERVE the TEXT of SCRIPTURE

READ John 15 and **MARK** every reference to *Jesus*.

John 15

1 *"I am the true vine, and My Father is the vinedresser.*

2 *"Every branch in Me that does not bear fruit, He takes away; and every branch that bears fruit, He prunes it so that it may bear more fruit.*

3 *"You are already clean because of the word which I have spoken to you.*

4 *"Abide in Me, and I in you. As the branch cannot bear fruit of itself unless it abides in the vine, so neither can you unless you abide in Me.*

5 *"I am the vine, you are the branches; he who abides in Me and I in him, he bears much fruit, for apart from Me you can do nothing.*

6 *"If anyone does not abide in Me, he is thrown away as a branch and dries up; and they gather them, and cast them into the fire and they are burned.*

7 *"If you abide in Me, and My words abide in you, ask whatever you wish, and it will be done for you.*

8 *"My Father is glorified by this, that you bear much fruit, and so prove to be My disciples.*

9 *"Just as the Father has loved Me, I have also loved you; abide in My love.*

10 *"If you keep My commandments, you will abide in My love; just as I have kept My Father's commandments and abide in His love.*

11 *"These things I have spoken to you so that My joy may be in you, and that your joy may be made full.*

12 *"This is My commandment, that you love one another, just as I have loved you.*

13 *"Greater love has no one than this, that one lay down his life for his friends.*

14 *"You are My friends if you do what I command you.*

15 *"No longer do I call you slaves, for the slave does not know what his master is doing; but I have called you friends, for all things that I have heard from My Father I have made known to you.*

16 *"You did not choose Me but I chose you, and appointed you that you would go and bear fruit, and that your fruit would remain, so that whatever you ask of the Father in My name He may give to you.*

17 *"This I command you, that you love one another.*

18 *"If the world hates you, you know that it has hated Me before it hated you.*

19 *"If you were of the world, the world would love its own; but because you are not of the world, but I chose you out of the world, because of this the world hates you.*

20 *"Remember the word that I said to you, 'A slave is not greater than his master.' If they persecuted Me, they will also persecute you; if they kept My word, they will keep yours also.*

21 *"But all these things they will do to you for My name's sake, because they do not know the One who sent Me.*

22 *"If I had not come and spoken to them, they would not have sin, but now they have no excuse for their sin.*

23 *"He who hates Me hates My Father also.*

24 *"If I had not done among them the works which no one else did, they would not have sin; but now they have both seen and hated Me and My Father as well.*

25 *"But they have done this to fulfill the word that is written in their Law, 'THEY HATED ME WITHOUT A CAUSE.'*

26 *"When the Helper comes, whom I will send to you from the Father, that is the Spirit of truth who proceeds from the Father, He will testify about Me,*

27 *and you will testify also, because you have been with Me from the beginning."*

FYI:

The Charger and the Phone

I'm a suburban girl—have been my whole life. I'm able to keep plants alive on my kitchen counter (for the most part!) but I don't understand agriculture firsthand. Grapes for me don't come from a vine; they come from a grocery store. Most plant-based metaphors are lost on me, like baseball or other types of metaphors may be lost on you. I understand them intellectually, but I don't *resonate* with them because they don't originate from "my world."

Metaphors help us understand by comparing the unusual and unclear with something typically common and crystal-clear. The clear helps us make sense of the unclear. So when Jesus talks about the vine and the branches, I get it, but not really firsthand.

The connection metaphor that totally resonates with me—and I'd put money down that you relate to this as well—is the cell phone and the power source. Now, the metaphor doesn't transfer perfectly (none do!). Still, as you read this chapter, keep in mind the feeling you have when you are by yourself, your phone is in the red zone and showing 3% battery life and you have no way of plugging in. How is that branch of a phone going to do when it is cut off from the vine of power?

JOY
FROM THE
UPPER ROOM
John 13-17

LESSON FOUR: **Abide in My Love**

DISCUSS with your GROUP or PONDER on your own . . .

What general observations did you make on John 15?

What location statement appears at the end of John 14? Do you think this might tie in with Jesus' teaching in John 15? If so, how?

Did you notice any repeating key words? (Remember to start with the "Whos?" when looking for key words and then move to the "Whats?") Write down the ones you recognize.

What main topics does Jesus address in this chapter? (You've probably recorded some of these as key words in answer to the previous question, right?!)

Does anything in this chapter stand out to you as potentially difficult? Explain.

What burning questions do you want answered?

LOOKING CLOSER . . .

Let's slow down as we look together at these life-changing words from Jesus!

OBSERVE the TEXT of SCRIPTURE

READ John 15:1-5 and **MARK** all of the "Who" references in a distinctive way (*Jesus, Father, branch*, etc.). Also **MARK** *abide(s)*.

John 15:1-5

1 *"I am the true vine, and My Father is the vinedresser.*

2 *"Every branch in Me that does not bear fruit, He takes away; and every branch that bears fruit, He prunes it so that it may bear more fruit.*

3 *"You are already clean because of the word which I have spoken to you.*

4 *"Abide in Me, and I in you. As the branch cannot bear fruit of itself unless it abides in the vine, so neither can you unless you abide in Me.*

5 *"I am the vine, you are the branches; he who abides in Me and I in him, he bears much fruit, for apart from Me you can do nothing."*

DISCUSS with your GROUP or PONDER on your own . . .

Who are the main characters in these verses and what is each compared to?

What is a branch supposed to do according to the text? How does it do this?

What happens if a branch is not connected to the vine? Can it accomplish its purpose? Why/why not?

ONE STEP FURTHER:

Short List: Jesus, 1–5
I hope you'll take the time to list what you learned about Jesus in these verses.

ONE STEP FURTHER:

Word Study: Takes Away
Take some time this week to find the Greek word translated "takes away." Then explore how else it is used in John and the rest of the New Testament. Record below what you discover.

Digging Deeper

Bearing Fruit

What is Jesus referring to when He talks about fruit-bearing in John 15? In order to help us interpret, take some time this week to explore other fruit/fruit-bearing references in the New Testament!

What Jesus says about fruit/fruit-bearing:

What Paul says about fruit/fruit-bearing:

What other New Testament writers say about fruit/fruit-bearing:

Summary:

ONE STEP FURTHER:

Word Study: Prunes

We only see the word "prunes" in the text one time, but the Greek word behind it appears twice and will help us as we interpret! See if you can find that other word this week and then compare how the Greek root is used in John 13 and John 15. Record your findings below. (Hint: One word is a verb, the other is an adjective.)

DISCUSS with your GROUP or PONDER on your own . . . (continued)

Compare John 15:3 with John 13:10-11 (see sidebar on right).

— Who is Jesus speaking to in John 15:3? Who are the ones who are clean?

— Who was Jesus speaking to in John 13:10-11? Who were the ones he said were clean and who was not clean?

OBSERVE the TEXT of SCRIPTURE

READ John 15:6-8. **UNDERLINE** references to those who do *not abide* and **CIRCLE** references to those who do *abide*.

John 15:6-8

6 *"If anyone does not abide in Me, he is thrown away as a branch and dries up; and they gather them, and cast them into the fire and they are burned.*

7 *"If you abide in Me, and My words abide in you, ask whatever you wish, and it will be done for you.*

8 *"My Father is glorified by this, that you bear much fruit, and so prove to be My disciples."*

DISCUSS with your GROUP or PONDER on your own . . .

Looking back to verses 4 and 5, what does a branch that abides in the vine do and how does it do it?

INDUCTIVE STUDY:

Compare Scripture with Scripture

A key tool we often use in inductive study is comparing Scripture with Scripture. In this case, we'll compare how John uses the word *katharos* (translated "clean") in John 15:3 and John 13:10-11 as one may help us understand the other.

John 15:3

"You are already clean because of the word which I have spoken to you."

John 13:10-11

Jesus said to him [Peter], "He who has bathed needs only to wash his feet, but is completely clean; and you are clean, but not all of you." For He knew the one who was betraying Him; for this reason He said, "Not all of you are clean."

FYI:

Use Colors If You Want To!

Just a reminder that if you like to use colored pencils or pens for marking the text, have at it! Sometimes I will ask you to UNDERLINE or CIRCLE because I want to make the instructions easy for those who are using only one color. Bottom line: mark in a way that helps you see key words easily. After all, that's the reason for marking—to help us better see what is happening in the text.

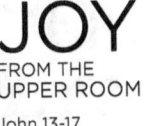

JOY
FROM THE
UPPER ROOM
John 13-17

LESSON FOUR: **Abide in My Love**

List what you learned in verses 6-8 about those who *don't* abide and those who *do* abide.

Those Who *Don't* Abide   **Those Who *Do* Abide**

ONE STEP FURTHER:

Word Study: Disciple

Take some time this week to look into the word "disciple." Find the Greek root and see how its noun and verb forms are used throughout the New Testament. Jot down your findings below and then answer this question: *According to the Bible, what is a disciple?*

Now, looking back over the verses and the lists you've made, what shows a person to be a disciple?

What did you learn about glorifying the Father? According to these verses, how can *you* glorify Him?

Think through this. Can you glorify the Father on your own? What is the only way you will be able to do this?

Now, let's get real here. Is there anything in these verses that makes you squirm—if not for yourself, then for people you know? Go ahead and write down your squirm-worthy question(s).

JOY
FROM THE
UPPER ROOM
John 13-17

Do you think we've already seen a no-fruit branch in John 13–15? Explain.

Before we move on to some cross-references, look back on this passage and identify the qualities of disciples.

Are these truths comforting to you? Explain.

Let's Look at Some Cross-References

Cross-references can help us understand Scripture better. When one passage leaves us with a head-scratching question, others can help us rule out or confirm possible interpretations. Let's see if we can find more clarity on the previous verses by examining some relevant cross-references.

In John 15:1-8 Jesus talks about two kinds of branches. One of the branches abides, bears fruit, proves that it is a disciple of Jesus, and thus glorifies God.

The other branch fails to abide, fails to bear fruit, and is thrown away and is eventually cast into the fire and burned.

The key question here is this: *Was the non-fruit-bearing branch ever a true believer?* Put another way: *Can a believer lose his or her salvation?*

Let's go to Scripture to find some answers!

OBSERVE the TEXT of SCRIPTURE

The "we" Paul uses in this section refers to himself and his readers, likely a mixture of Jewish and Gentile believers.

READ Romans 8:28-39 and **MARK** references to *God*. **UNDERLINE** everything that God does.

Romans 8:28-39

28 And we know that God causes all things to work together for good to those who love God, to those who are called according to His purpose.

INDUCTIVE TOOLS:

Paying Attention to the Clear

When we run across something in Scripture that confuses us, it's easy to throw our hands in the air and start running the other direction. Full disclosure: I've done that from time to time. Most notably, I did it when I was in the fifth grade and stumbled across Romans 9 while reading the book of Romans in AWANA. Running away from it didn't help. What did help was looking straight at it in college and trying to determine what was clear about the passage.

Looking right at the passage, asking God to teach you, and then focusing first on what truth is absolutely clear will get you a long ways down the road as you seek to interpret a passage you think is difficult.

Sometimes what is clear will help you figure out what is unclear. Other times, what you clearly learn about God will be enough to help you tolerate mystery.

The more I know my heavenly Father, the more mystery I can tolerate because I know He is absolutely trustworthy to handle even the things I do not understand.

LESSON FOUR: **Abide in My Love**

29 For those whom He foreknew, He also predestined to become *conformed to the image of His Son, so that He would be the firstborn among many brethren;*

30 and these whom He predestined, He also called; and these whom He called, He also justified; and these whom He justified, He also glorified.

31 What then shall we say to these things? If God is for us, who is against us?

32 He who did not spare His own Son, but delivered Him over for us all, how will He not also with Him freely give us all things?

33 Who will bring a charge against God's elect? God is the one who justifies;

34 who is the one who condemns? Christ Jesus is He who died, yes, rather who was raised, who is at the right hand of God, who also intercedes for us.

35 Who will separate us from the love of Christ? Will tribulation, or distress, or persecution, or famine, or nakedness, or peril, or sword?

36 Just as it is written, "FOR YOUR SAKE WE ARE BEING PUT TO DEATH ALL DAY LONG; WE WERE CONSIDERED AS SHEEP TO BE SLAUGHTERED."

37 But in all these things we overwhelmingly conquer through Him who loved us.

38 For I am convinced that neither death, nor life, nor angels, nor principalities, nor things present, nor things to come, nor powers,

39 nor height, nor depth, nor any other created thing, will be able to separate us from the love of God, which is in Christ Jesus our Lord.

DISCUSS with your GROUP or PONDER on your own . . .

What does this text teach us about God? What encouragement can this give you today?

What specifically does He do according to this passage? Note the verbs that you underlined.

How do these actions affect believers?

According to Romans 8, can a person who has been foreknown, predestined, called, justified, and glorified ever be separated from the love of God in Christ? Explain.

What difference can knowing the truths of Romans 8 make as you encounter difficulties in life?

How can Romans 8:28-39 help us understand John 15:1-8?

OBSERVE the TEXT of SCRIPTURE

The "we" Paul uses in this section refers to himself and his fellow-believing readers.

READ Ephesians 1:3-6 and **MARK** references to *God* and to *us.*

Ephesians 1:3-6

3 *Blessed be the God and Father of our Lord Jesus Christ, who has blessed us with every spiritual blessing in the heavenly places in Christ,*

4 *just as He chose us in Him before the foundation of the world, that we would be holy and blameless before Him. In love*

5 *He predestined us to adoption as sons through Jesus Christ to Himself, according to the kind intention of His will,*

6 *to the praise of the glory of His grace, which He freely bestowed on us in the Beloved.*

DISCUSS with your GROUP or PONDER on your own . . .

According to these verses, what has God done for us and why has He done it?

ONE STEP FURTHER:

Other "Keeping" Verses?
Are there other verses that come to mind for you when considering God's power to "keep" those who belong to Him? This is a verse category that is important to know, especially during difficult and trying times. Write down those that come to mind, and if you have a little extra time, see if you can discover a few more. Record your findings below.

LESSON FOUR: **Abide in My Love**

What does Jesus Christ have to do with God's actions toward us?

When did God choose us? What does this say about our part in it?

How can this help us with John 15:1-8?

OBSERVE the TEXT of SCRIPTURE

In these latter verses of John 10, Jesus responds to the Jews' demand that He tell them if He is the Christ.

READ John 10:27-29 and **MARK** references to Jesus' *sheep* (remember to mark *them* and *they* as appropriate).

John 10:27-29

27 *"My sheep hear My voice, and I know them, and they follow Me;*

28 *and I give eternal life to* them, *and they will never perish; and no one will snatch* them *out of My hand.*

29 *"My Father, who has given* them *to Me, is greater than all; and no one is able to snatch* them *out of the Father's hand."*

DISCUSS with your GROUP or PONDER on your own . . .

What does Jesus say about His sheep in these verses?

What specifically does Jesus say cannot happen to His sheep? How can this bring comfort to you if you are one of His sheep?

How can this help us with John 15:1-8?

OBSERVE the TEXT of SCRIPTURE

As we move back to the main text of John 15, I'd love for you to mark a few extra words this time as there are so many that are important. Don't worry, I'm not trending the direction of marking everything—this section is just dense with words that matter.

READ John 15:9-17. Then **MARK** in a distinctive fashion the following words: *love/loved*, *abide/remain* (yup, same Greek word), *command/commandments*, and *joy!*

John 15:9-17

9   *"Just as the Father has loved Me, I have also loved you; abide in My love.*

10 *"If you keep My commandments, you will abide in My love; just as I have kept My Father's commandments and abide in His love.*

11 *"These things I have spoken to you so that My joy may be in you, and that your joy may be made full.*

12 *"This is My commandment, that you love one another, just as I have loved you.*

13 *"Greater love has no one than this, that one lay down his life for his friends.*

14 *"You are My friends if you do what I command you.*

15 *"No longer do I call you slaves, for the slave does not know what his master is doing; but I have called you friends, for all things that I have heard from My Father I have made known to you.*

16 *"You did not choose Me but I chose you, and appointed you that you would go and bear fruit, and that your fruit would remain, so that whatever you ask of the Father in My name He may give to you.*

17 *"This I command you, that you love one another."*

ONE STEP FURTHER:

Word Study: Joy

Take some time this week to explore the word "joy." What Greek word does it translate? How does John use it? How do we see it used elsewhere in the New Testament? Record your findings below.

JOY
FROM THE
UPPER ROOM
John 13-17

LESSON FOUR: **Abide in My Love**

DISCUSS with your GROUP or PONDER on your own . . .

What does Jesus say about love in these verses? Note what love has to do with the Father, Jesus, and His disciples.

What do commandments have to do with love?

Earlier in John 15, Jesus told the disciples to abide "in Him." What does He tell them to abide "in" in this section? How are they to do this? How had Jesus modeled this?

In verse 11 Jesus tells His disciples why he has spoken "these things" to them. What are "these things" and what do they have to do with Jesus' joy and ours?

Have you ever considered Jesus' joy? According to Hebrews 12:1-3 (left sidebar), what role did joy play in Jesus' life as He faced and endured the cross? What can we learn from this? How specifically can you apply this in your life today?

What does Jesus specifically command His disciples in verses 12 and 17?

How do you think the Church as a whole is doing with this commandment? How are you doing individually? Where might you need to better submit to the Spirit's work in this area?

What does Jesus say about friends in verses 13-15? How has He shown (and how will He show) His friendship to the disciples? How will they show that they are His friends?

Is there anything from Jesus' teaching in John 15 that you need to apply to your friendships today? Be as specific as possible in your response.

Finally, according to verse 16, what has Jesus already done for the disciples? How does this compare with the cross-references we looked at earlier? How can this bring peace in difficult days? How can it bring you peace?

@THE END OF THE DAY . . .

John 15 delivers truth on joy and friendship, abiding and obeying, loving and bearing fruit. Spend some time reviewing what you have learned and asking God what truth from John 15 you most need to apply today . . . then write that one truth below.

LESSON FIVE: **Abide in My Love**

Not of This World

"If you were of the world, the world would love its own; but because you are not of the world, but I chose you out of the world, because of this the world hates you."
—Jesus, John 15:19

If the world seems hostile to you, if you feel like "the enemy" half the time and out of sorts the other, be encouraged. Jesus warned His disciples of this before He left. "But wait," you say, "hasn't the world become more calloused, more hateful, more difficult in the past half-century? Hasn't common decency all but ceased in today's digital age?"

Perhaps it has changed for the worse compared to what some of us have witnessed in our lifetimes—some years of which we have lived under a primarily Judeo-Christian ethic—but the world's hatred of Jesus' followers has a long history—a history going back to the time of Jesus Himself. Although Scripture does not record how Jesus' closest followers died, historical evidence suggests that all of the disciples save John died martyrs' deaths. The early church father, Tertullian, records that John survived being boiled in oil.

Opposition to God and His people goes way back . . . all the way back to the Garden.

 FYI:

Opposition and Persecution
I recently finished a fascinating book called *The Insanity of God* that chronicles the stories of men and women around the world who have persevered through persecution for the Gospel of Jesus Christ. If you doubt that the cross brings persecution, let this book open your eyes to what our brothers and sisters in Christ around the world have endured and are enduring. It re-framed my thinking and I recommend it highly to you.

ONE STEP FURTHER:

Read and Re-Read

You can't read God's Word too much! If you have time today, instead of just overviewing John 15, go ahead and re-read John 13–17 and soak in the entire passage that we're studying! Record anything that you'd specifically like to remember below. Keep it short!

LESSON FIVE: **Not of This World**

REMEMBERING

Summarize in a paragraph or two what you've learned so far in John 13, 14, and 15.

Now, take a moment to assess your thoughts on memorizing. If you're memorizing, how is it going? Are you finding it beneficial? If you've decided against it, are you comfortable with that decision? (Not trying to be a pest, but I don't want you to give up before even praying about it!)

OVERVIEW JOHN 15

While we'll be focusing on John 15:17-27 this week, let's read the whole chapter again before diving more deeply into the second half.

OBSERVE the TEXT of SCRIPTURE

READ John 15 and **PICK** a word or two of interest to **MARK**.

John 15

1   *"I am the true vine, and My Father is the vinedresser.*

2   *"Every branch in Me that does not bear fruit, He takes away; and every branch that bears fruit, He prunes it so that it may bear more fruit.*

3   *"You are already clean because of the word which I have spoken to you.*

4   *"Abide in Me, and I in you. As the branch cannot bear fruit of itself unless it abides in the vine, so neither can you unless you abide in Me.*

5   *"I am the vine, you are the branches; he who abides in Me and I in him, he bears much fruit, for apart from Me you can do nothing.*

6　*"If anyone does not abide in Me, he is thrown away as a branch and dries up; and they gather them, and cast them into the fire and they are burned.*

7　*"If you abide in Me, and My words abide in you, ask whatever you wish, and it will be done for you.*

8　*"My Father is glorified by this, that you bear much fruit, and so prove to be My disciples.*

9　*"Just as the Father has loved Me, I have also loved you; abide in My love.*

10　*"If you keep My commandments, you will abide in My love; just as I have kept My Father's commandments and abide in His love.*

11　*"These things I have spoken to you so that My joy may be in you, and that your joy may be made full.*

12　*"This is My commandment, that you love one another, just as I have loved you.*

13　*"Greater love has no one than this, that one lay down his life for his friends.*

14　*"You are My friends if you do what I command you.*

15　*"No longer do I call you slaves, for the slave does not know what his master is doing; but I have called you friends, for all things that I have heard from My Father I have made known to you.*

16　*"You did not choose Me but I chose you, and appointed you that you would go and bear fruit, and that your fruit would remain, so that whatever you ask of the Father in My name He may give to you.*

17　*"This I command you, that you love one another.*

18　*"If the world hates you, you know that it has hated Me before it hated you.*

19　*"If you were of the world, the world would love its own; but because you are not of the world, but I chose you out of the world, because of this the world hates you.*

20　*"Remember the word that I said to you, 'A slave is not greater than his master.' If they persecuted Me, they will also persecute you; if they kept My word, they will keep yours also.*

21　*"But all these things they will do to you for My name's sake, because they do not know the One who sent Me.*

22　*"If I had not come and spoken to them, they would not have sin, but now they have no excuse for their sin.*

23　*"He who hates Me hates My Father also.*

24　*"If I had not done among them the works which no one else did, they would not have sin; but now they have both seen and hated Me and My Father as well.*

25　*"But they have done this to fulfill the word that is written in their Law, 'THEY HATED ME WITHOUT A CAUSE.'*

26　*"When the Helper comes, whom I will send to you from the Father, that is the Spirit of truth who proceeds from the Father, He will testify about Me,*

27　*and you will testify also, because you have been with Me from the beginning."*

INDUCTIVE TOOLS:

Context is King!
Remember as you study that context is king because it rules in matters of interpretation. As you study verse by verse and chapter by chapter, remember and compare what you're seeing with what you've already observed and studied! I think you'll be amazed at how many questions are answered right in the text when we slow down enough to notice.

JOY
FROM THE
UPPER ROOM
John 13–17

LESSON FIVE: **Not of This World**

DISCUSS with your GROUP or PONDER on your own . . .

What word(s) did you select and why?

List what you learned by marking the word or words.

LOOKING CLOSER . . .

Let's look more closely at verses 17-27. And, yes, verse 17 was in last week's lesson, but we're overlapping on purpose. Thanks for noticing! ;)

OBSERVE the TEXT of SCRIPTURE

READ John 15:17-25 and **MARK** every reference to *love* and *hate*.

John 15:17-25

17 *"This I command you, that you love one another.*

18 *"If the world hates you, you know that it has hated Me before it hated you.*

19 *"If you were of the world, the world would love its own; but because you are not of the world, but I chose you out of the world, because of this the world hates you.*

20 *"Remember the word that I said to you, 'A slave is not greater than his master.' If they persecuted Me, they will also persecute you; if they kept My word, they will keep yours also.*

21 *"But all these things they will do to you for My name's sake, because they do not know the One who sent Me.*

22 *"If I had not come and spoken to them, they would not have sin, but now they have no excuse for their sin.*

23 *"He who hates Me hates My Father also.*

JOY
FROM THE
UPPER ROOM
John 13-17

24 *"If I had not done among them the works which no one else did, they would not have sin; but now they have both seen and hated Me and My Father as well.*

25 *"But* they have done this *to fulfill the word that is written in their Law, 'THEY HATED ME WITHOUT A CAUSE.' "*

DISCUSS with your GROUP or PONDER on your own . . .

Based on Jesus' command in verses 12 and 17, what should characterize His followers specifically?

Are there times when it is easier for you to show love toward those outside of the body of Christ as opposed to those inside of it? Explain your answer.

Now—and I know this may be uncomfortable—think of a time when the "love one another" command was difficult between you and another person. Got it? Write down the core issue but leave names out.

Here's where it will be hard. Put yourself into the other person's shoes for a moment and consider what in your life may be making it difficult for others to obey "love one another" with regard to you. Go ahead and write it down.

ONE STEP FURTHER:

Word Study: World

As in English, words in Greek can have different meanings or shades of meaning depending on context. If you have some time this week, see what you can discover about the word "world." What is the Greek word that John uses? How did he use this word in John 15, in his Gospel, and in his other writings?

Then answer this question: *Who does Jesus say will hate the Christian? What implications does this have for how I think and live?*

JOY
FROM THE
UPPER ROOM
John 13-17

LESSON FIVE: **Not of This World**

Digging Deeper

"For My Name's Sake"

Paul tells us in Philippians 2:10-11 that "at the name of Jesus EVERY KNEE WILL BOW, of those who are in heaven and on earth and under the earth, and that every tongue will confess that Jesus Christ is Lord, to the glory of God the Father."

In John 14–17 this name is associated with everything from answered prayers to persecution. Take some time this week to examine the 12 uses of the Greek word *onoma* ("name") in these chapters, then its uses in John's other writings and the rest of the New Testament. This will help provide much needed background for answering some of our other questions!

John 14–17

Other uses in John's Gospel (summarize)

Uses in 1, 2, 3 John (summarize)

Uses in Revelation (summarize)

Other New Testament Uses (summarize)

Summarize what you learned about *onoma*. How does this help us in better understanding John 14–17?

How are you doing at loving other believers who think differently than you? Let's get a bit specific here. What topic throws a rain cloud on your day if someone starts arguing with you about it? Why does the topic upset you?

How do you typically respond? Is there a more biblical or Christlike way you can respond in the future? Bring some specific verses to bear on this. We'll talk more on the "why" of this later in John 17!

Although Christ's followers will find love in the Church, how does this compare with what His followers will encounter in the world?

List what you learned by marking the word "hate."

Who does the world hate and why?

Who does the world love and why?

How can Jesus' words encourage you when you find yourself neck-deep in the world's hate? Write down specific encouragements from the text.

How do you typically respond to the world's hate? Will these verses change your responses going forward? What truth or truths do you align with?

INDUCTIVE STUDY:

Unclear in Light of Clear
Remember that when we find something in Scripture that is seems unclear we always interpret it in light of what is clear. In order to properly handle 15:22 and 24 we need to start by considering what the Bible clearly teaches about sin. Take some time today to record key verses that address the biblical view of sin.

OBSERVE the TEXT of SCRIPTURE

Yes, we're overlapping here a bit once again, but I want to keep these four verses in front of our eyes as we look at them more specifically.

READ John 15:22-25 and **MARK** every reference to *sin*.

John 15:22-25

22 *"If I had not come and spoken to them, they would not have sin, but now they have no excuse for their sin.*

23 *"He who hates Me hates My Father also.*

24 *"If I had not done among them the works which no one else did, they would not have sin; but now they have both seen and hated Me and My Father as well.*

25 *"But they have done this to fulfill the word that is written in their Law, 'THEY HATED ME WITHOUT A CAUSE.' "*

DISCUSS with your GROUP or PONDER on your own . . .

Who are the "them/they" that Jesus refers to in verses 22-25? (Pay attention to verse 25 as you answer.)

JOY
FROM THE
UPPER ROOM
John 13-17

LESSON FIVE: **Not of This World**

What does Jesus say about sin in these verses? Write down specific statements from the text.

FYI:

Grammar Nerds Unite!

In John 15:22 and 24 Jesus makes two statements about situations that didn't happen. Grammar nerds—like myself—call these "contrary-to-fact conditional clauses." Before you roll your eyes to the back of your head, let's put this grammar stuff into street-level English.

In verse 22, Jesus says that if He hadn't come and spoken to "them, they would not have sin . . . ." But He did speak and they rejected His words, sinning the new sin of hating Him and His Father.

Similarly, in verse 24, Jesus shows that the people who have been claiming to love the Father have actively rejected Him (and thus the Father) even after seeing the works He did firsthand.

If He hadn't spoken truth to them, if He hadn't done works among them, they would not have sinned the sin of rejecting these things . . . not *not-sinned-at-all*.

Both verses 22 and 24 contain "contrary-to-fact conditional clauses" (explained in the sidebar on p. 71). They refer to two things that did not happen. What does the text say did happen and what were the resulting conditions?

Considering Jesus from a Jewish perspective, who did the Jewish people reject?

According to this text, is it possible for anyone (Jew or Gentile) to reject Jesus and love God? Explain.

How do people in your life respond to Jesus? Do they respond differently to His name than to the more general term "God"? What do you make of this?

Finally, what role does sin play in understanding the Gospel? (Spoiler: We'll soon see Who convicts of sin, righteousness, and judgment and testifies to Jesus!)

OBSERVE the TEXT of SCRIPTURE

READ John 15:26-27 and **MARK** in distinct ways every reference to *the Father, the Son,* and *the Holy Spirit.*

John 15:26-27

26 *"When the Helper comes, whom I will send to you from the Father, that is the Spirit of truth who proceeds from the Father, He will testify about Me,*

27 *and you will testify also, because you have been with Me from the beginning.*

DISCUSS with your GROUP or PONDER on your own . . .

What did you learn about the Father in these verses?

What did you learn about Jesus?

What did you learn about the Helper? Who is He and what does He do?

How do each of the members of the Trinity interact with each other?

Who does Jesus say will testify about Him and why?

ONE STEP FURTHER:

Word Study: Testify

Take some time to find the Greek word that is translated "testify" in John 15:26-27. When you find it, you'll be able to see a recognizable English word in it! Then see what else you can discover about John's use of the word and how else it is used throughout the New Testament. Record your findings below.

LESSON FIVE: **Not of This World**

How do you testify about Jesus in your life and in your world?

Who testified about Jesus to you?

@THE END OF THE DAY . . .

Take some time to pray and consider how you will specifically apply what you've learned this week. When you are done, write down a one-sentence summary of how you can respond in submission to God's Word this week.

An Unexpected Advantage!

"But I tell you the truth, it is to your advantage that I go away . . . ."
—Jesus, John 16:7a

What do you do when grief has you pinned against a wall? When every hope seems lost? When tomorrow's forecast—not just your imagination of it!—is darker than today's? What do you do?

Hearing the news of Jesus' impending departure and facing the world's growing hatred toward them, the disciples' hearts filled with sorrow. It's understandable, don't you think? What would they do without Jesus there to teach them, lead them, guide them, protect and encourage them? What kind of life would they be left to when He was gone and Jewish leaders redirected their fury toward them?

Against their fear of loss and abandonment, Jesus injects the hope of something more than they—or we!—could ever dream of, an advantage, the Helper, the Spirit of truth! With darkness looming, Jesus promises to send His Light!

LESSON SIX: **An Unexpected Advantage!**

REMEMBERING

This week, let's review chapter by chapter. Take some time to think through what you've learned in John 13, 14, and 15. In the first column, write down what you remember off the top of your head without looking. Then, in the second column, after reviewing, write down another way to remember the content or application for the chapters.

FYI:

Don't Overthink This!
I'm not fishing for a "right" answer on this review section. I want you to consider, to meditate, to think on what you've been learning so you can call it to mind in different ways. There are countless ways we can categorize content. If your first column focuses more on facts, perhaps you'll want to make the second column more application-oriented (or vice versa!). If you wrote a simple summary of each chapter in column one, you may want to pick a key verse to remember for each chapter in column two. Bottomline: This is to continue to push you back to the text to look at it from various angles and to think about it more and more. The more you think about how to remember it, you know what's happening, right? Before you know it, you're remembering it!

From Memory	A New Reminder
John 13	
John 14	
John 15	

OVERVIEW JOHN 16

You know the drill already, right? Let's read John 16 to overview it before focusing on smaller segments of the chapter!

OBSERVE the TEXT of SCRIPTURE

READ John 16 and **MARK** every reference to *Jesus*.

John 16

1   *"These things I have spoken to you so that you may be kept from stumbling.*

2   *"They will make you outcasts from the synagogue, but an hour is coming for everyone who kills you to think that he is offering service to God.*

3   *"These things they will do because they have not known the Father or Me.*

4   *"But these things I have spoken to you, so that when their hour comes, you may remember that I told you of them. These things I did not say to you at the beginning, because I was with you.*

5   *"But now I am going to Him who sent Me; and none of you asks Me, 'Where are You going?'*

6   *"But because I have said these things to you, sorrow has filled your heart.*

7   *"But I tell you the truth, it is to your advantage that I go away; for if I do not go away, the Helper will not come to you; but if I go, I will send Him to you.*

8   *"And He, when He comes, will convict the world concerning sin and righteousness and judgment;*

9   *concerning sin, because they do not believe in Me;*

10 *and concerning righteousness, because I go to the Father and you no longer see Me;*

11 *and concerning judgment, because the ruler of this world has been judged.*

12 *"I have many more things to say to you, but you cannot bear them now.*

13 *"But when He, the Spirit of truth, comes, He will guide you into all the truth; for He will not speak on His own initiative, but whatever He hears, He will speak; and He will disclose to you what is to come.*

14 *"He will glorify Me, for He will take of Mine and will disclose it to you.*

15 *"All things that the Father has are Mine; therefore I said that He takes of Mine and will disclose it to you.*

16 *"A little while, and you will no longer see Me; and again a little while, and you will see Me."*

17 *Some of His disciples then said to one another, "What is this thing He is telling us, 'A little while, and you will not see Me; and again a little while, and you will see Me'; and, 'because I go to the Father'?"*

18 *So they were saying, "What is this that He says, 'A little while'? We do not know what He is talking about."*

19 *Jesus knew that they wished to question Him, and He said to them, "Are you deliberating together about this, that I said, 'A little while, and you will not see Me, and again a little while, and you will see Me'?*

JOY
FROM THE
UPPER ROOM
John 13-17

LESSON SIX: **An Unexpected Advantage!**

20 "Truly, truly, I say to you, that you will weep and lament, but the world will rejoice; you will grieve, but your grief will be turned into joy.

21 "Whenever a woman is in labor she has pain, because her hour has come; but when she gives birth to the child, she no longer remembers the anguish because of the joy that a child has been born into the world.

22 "Therefore you too have grief now; but I will see you again, and your heart will rejoice, and no one will take your joy away from you.

23 "In that day you will not question Me about anything. Truly, truly, I say to you, if you ask the Father for anything in My name, He will give it to you.

24 "Until now you have asked for nothing in My name; ask and you will receive, so that your joy may be made full.

25 "These things I have spoken to you in figurative language; an hour is coming when I will no longer speak to you in figurative language, but will tell you plainly of the Father.

26 "In that day you will ask in My name, and I do not say to you that I will request of the Father on your behalf;

27 for the Father Himself loves you, because you have loved Me and have believed that I came forth from the Father.

28 "I came forth from the Father and have come into the world; I am leaving the world again and going to the Father."

29 His disciples said, "Lo, now You are speaking plainly and are not using a figure of speech.

30 "Now we know that You know all things, and have no need for anyone to question You; by this we believe that You came from God."

31 Jesus answered them, "Do you now believe?

32 "Behold, an hour is coming, and has already come, for you to be scattered, each to his own home, and to leave Me alone; and yet I am not alone, because the Father is with Me.

33 "These things I have spoken to you, so that in Me you may have peace. In the world you have tribulation, but take courage; I have overcome the world."

DISCUSS with your GROUP or PONDER on your own . . .

What is the general context of this chapter? What has happened up to this point?

What are your initial observations?

What did you learn about Jesus in this chapter? List the most important truths you discovered along with their references.

ONE STEP FURTHER:

Jesus List
Want to compile a more complete list about Jesus from John 16? Here's the room to do it!

What other key words did you note?

What big questions that stand out to you in this chapter do you want answered?

LOOKING CLOSER . . .

With so many "things" to look at in this section, let's get to it!

OBSERVE the TEXT of SCRIPTURE

READ John 16:1-4 and **MARK** in distinctive ways references to the phrases *these things* and *so that*

John 16:1-4

1 "These things I have spoken to you so that you may be kept from stumbling.

2 "They will make you outcasts from the synagogue, but an hour is coming for everyone who kills you to think that he is offering service to God.

3 "These things they will do because they have not known the Father or Me.

4 "But these things I have spoken to you, so that when their hour comes, you may remember that I told you of them. These things I did not say to you at the beginning, because I was with you."

LESSON SIX: **An Unexpected Advantage!**

DISCUSS with your GROUP or PONDER on your own . . .

What do "these things" in verses 1 and 4 refer to? What has Jesus spoken about and for what purposes?

Why hadn't He spoken about "these things" earlier?

What threats will the disciples face?

Who will come against them? How do you know from the text?

What do these people think they know about God? What do their actions reveal?

What specifics does Jesus tell them?

Have you ever been an "outcast" because of your relationship to Jesus? What do you make of this?

In what ways does the world come against Jesus' followers in your culture and around the world today?

How do you think these words helped the disciples then? How can you apply them today?

Cross-References

In one of His "so that" statements, Jesus says that He has spoken "so that" His disciples "may be kept from stumbling" (16:1). The Greek verb *skandalizo* ("stumbling") is also translated "falling away" (ESV) and "fall away" (NIV).

In the following passages we'll be focusing on the use of this word in a couple of other Gospel passages. You can summarize what you find in the **One Step Further** sidebar on the following page.

OBSERVE the TEXT of SCRIPTURE

As we look at the Parable of the Sower, you may want to read the entire account of it in Matthew 13:1-23 in your Bible. The text below includes the parable (vv. 1-9) and Jesus' interpretation of it for His disciples (vv. 18-23). In between (vv. 10-17), the disciples ask Jesus why He speaks in parables. That, my friends, is a study for another day! In this passage, as we're looking for more information on the usage of *skandalizo*, we'll be focusing on the seed that falls on the rocky place.

READ Matthew 13:18-23 and **MARK** every reference to *falls away*.

Matthew 13:1-9, 18-23

1   *That day Jesus went out of the house and was sitting by the sea.*

2   *And large crowds gathered to Him, so He got into a boat and sat down, and the whole crowd was standing on the beach.*

JOY
FROM THE
UPPER ROOM
John 13-17

ONE STEP FURTHER:

Word Studies: *Skandalizo*

Take some time this week to see how this Greek word is used in John's writings, the Synoptic Gospels, and the rest of the New Testament. Record your findings below.

3 And He spoke many things to them in parables, saying, "Behold, the sower went out to sow;

4 and as he sowed, some seeds fell beside the road, and the birds came and ate them up.

5 "Others fell on the rocky places, where they did not have much soil; and immediately they sprang up, because they had no depth of soil.

6 "But when the sun had risen, they were scorched; and because they had no root, they withered away.

7 "Others fell among the thorns, and the thorns came up and choked them out.

8 "And others fell on the good soil and yielded a crop, some a hundredfold, some sixty, and some thirty.

9 "He who has ears, let him hear."

18 "Hear then the parable of the sower.

19 "When anyone hears the word of the kingdom and does not understand it, the evil one comes and snatches away what has been sown in his heart. This is the one on whom seed was sown beside the road.

20 "The one on whom seed was sown on the rocky places, this is the man who hears the word and immediately receives it with joy;

21 yet he has no firm root in himself, but is only temporary, and when affliction or persecution arises because of the word, immediately he falls away.

22 "And the one on whom seed was sown among the thorns, this is the man who hears the word, and the worry of the world and the deceitfulness of wealth choke the word, and it becomes unfruitful.

23 "And the one on whom seed was sown on the good soil, this is the man who hears the word and understands it; who indeed bears fruit and brings forth, some a hundredfold, some sixty, and some thirty."

DISCUSS with your GROUP or PONDER on your own . . .

What four situations or conditions does Jesus describe in these verses?

Let's focus on the seed thrown "on the rocky places":

What happens initially? How does the plant look at the outset? Would you bet on it? Why/why not?

What eventually happens to the plant in the rocky place in the initial parable?

How does Jesus explain this to the disciples in verses 21-22? How do affliction (Greek: *thlipsis*) and persecution (Greek: *diogmos*) affect this plant?

Compare this with Romans 5:1-5 (see sidebar). What does affliction or tribulation produce in the life of one who has been justified by faith in Jesus?

How have you seen tribulation work in your life? Does knowing truth help you face it?

Now, think back to Jesus' words in John 16:1. Knowing that His disciples will face hard times imminently, what has Jesus told them to keep them from stumbling or falling away?

How can this help you today? What specific truth can you apply in your life?

FYI:

Truth from Romans 5

Therefore, having been justified by faith, we have peace with God through our Lord Jesus Christ, through whom also we have obtained our introduction by faith into this grace in which we stand; and we exult in hope of the glory of God. And not only this, but we also exult in our tribulations [Greek: thlipsis] knowing that tribulation [thlipsis] brings about perseverance; and perseverance, proven character; and proven character, hope; and hope does not disappoint, because the love of God has been poured out within our hearts through the Holy Spirit who was given to us.

—Romans 5:1-5

FYI:

Truth from Paul to Timothy

Indeed, all who desire to live godly in Christ Jesus will be persecuted.

—2 Timothy 3:12

JOY
FROM THE
UPPER ROOM
John 13-17

LESSON SIX: **An Unexpected Advantage!**

OBSERVE the TEXT of SCRIPTURE

As we continue to look at the word *skandalizo*, we'll see that while Jesus has spoken words so that His disciples won't fall away completely, He knows that all of them are heading for a trip up. We've already looked at Jesus and Peter's conversation at the end of John 13, but now let's look at a similar passage from Matthew.

READ Matthew 26:26-35 and **MARK** every reference to *fall away*.

Matthew 26:26-35

26 *While they were eating, Jesus took some bread, and after a blessing, He broke it and gave it to the disciples, and said, "Take, eat; this is My body."*

27 *And when He had taken a cup and given thanks, He gave it to them, saying, "Drink from it, all of you;*

28 *for this is My blood of the covenant, which is poured out for many for forgiveness of sins.*

29 *"But I say to you, I will not drink of this fruit of the vine from now on until that day when I drink it new with you in My Father's kingdom."*

30 *After singing a hymn, they went out to the Mount of Olives.*

31 *Then Jesus said to them, "You will all fall away because of Me this night, for it is written, 'I WILL STRIKE DOWN THE SHEPHERD, AND THE SHEEP OF THE FLOCK SHALL BE SCATTERED.'*

32 *"But after I have been raised, I will go ahead of you to Galilee."*

33 *But Peter said to Him, "Even though all may fall away because of You, I will never fall away."*

34 *Jesus said to him, "Truly I say to you that this very night, before a rooster crows, you will deny Me three times."*

35 *Peter said to Him, "Even if I have to die with You, I will not deny You." All the disciples said the same thing too.*

DISCUSS with your GROUP or PONDER on your own . . .

What is the setting of this passage? Who is Jesus speaking to? What is happening?

When and where does Jesus say He will drink again of the fruit of the vine? With whom will He drink it? What does this tell us about those He is drinking with?

FYI:

Quoting Zechariah

Jesus quotes Zechariah 13:7 when He tells His disciples that they will leave Him before reuniting with Him in Galilee after His resurrection. Here is more of the passage for context.

6 "And one will say to him, 'What are these wounds between your arms?' Then he will say, 'Those with which I was wounded in the house of my friends.'

7 "Awake, O sword, against My Shepherd, and against the man, My Associate," declares the LORD of hosts. "Strike the Shepherd that the sheep may be scattered; and I will turn My hand against the little ones.

8 "It will come about in all the land," declares the LORD, "that two parts in it will be cut off and perish; but the third will be left in it.

9 "And I will bring the third part through the fire, refine them as silver is refined, and test them as gold is tested. They will call on My name, and I will answer them; I will say, 'They are My people,' and they will say, 'The LORD is my God.' "

—Zechariah 13:6-9

List what you learned by marking the phrase "fall away." Who does Jesus say will fall away and why?

How do the disciples respond to this?

What will change for them according to Jesus' words in John 14–16?

How does the Holy Spirit change the way the you live? Is most of your life spent yielding to Him or quenching Him? Explain.

OBSERVE the TEXT of SCRIPTURE

Let's look at John 16:5-15.

READ John 16:5-15 and **MARK** every reference to the *Helper* (including other names for Him) and **UNDERLINE** everything that He does.

John 16:5-15

5 *"But now I am going to Him who sent Me; and none of you asks Me, 'Where are You going?'*

6 *"But because I have said these things to you, sorrow has filled your heart.*

7 *"But I tell you the truth, it is to your advantage that I go away; for if I do not go away, the Helper will not come to you; but if I go, I will send Him to you.*

8 *"And He, when He comes, will convict the world concerning sin and righteousness and judgment;*

9 *concerning sin, because they do not believe in Me;*

LESSON SIX: **An Unexpected Advantage!**

10 *and concerning righteousness, because I go to the Father and you no longer see Me;*

11 *and concerning judgment, because the ruler of this world has been judged.*

12 *"I have many more things to say to you, but you cannot bear them now.*

13 *"But when He, the Spirit of truth, comes, He will guide you into all the truth; for He will not speak on His own initiative, but whatever He hears, He will speak; and He will disclose to you what is to come.*

14 *"He will glorify Me, for He will take of Mine and will disclose it to you.*

15 *"All things that the Father has are Mine; therefore I said that He takes of Mine and will disclose it to you."*

DISCUSS with your GROUP or PONDER on your own . . .

While Jesus has been telling the disciples that He is going away and going to prepare a place for them, what have they failed to ask Him?

What does Jesus recognize about the disciples' emotional condition? Why are they in this emotional state?

What encouraging truth does Jesus bring to the situation?

Why will Jesus' departure work in the disciples' favor?

ONE STEP FURTHER:

Jesus, the Man

If you have some time this week, see what you can find out about Jesus' humanity. What scriptures show Him experiencing fully human emotions and responses? Record what you discover below.

While Jesus was fully God, He was also fully human. Sometimes we forget that and think that His deity somehow made His humanity less real as though temptations were less for Him than for us because He was also fully divine. The opposite, I think, is true. Because Jesus never succumbed to sin, He felt the full weight of temptation in ways that you and I never have and never will!

Digging Deeper

The Father, the Son, the Spirit

Another of Scripture's great mysteries is the Trinity—Father, Son, Holy Spirit, one God, three Persons. While we will never be able to fully explain it, we can observe, consider, and learn.

Take some time this week to record what you learned in John 16 about the Father, the Son, and the Holy Spirit and their relationships with one another.

Father:

Son:

Spirit:

Some ways they relate with one another:

LESSON SIX: **An Unexpected Advantage!**

Have you ever thought, "If I had lived in Old Testament times when God did things like show up in a burning bush, it would have been easier to believe" or "If I had seen Jesus perform miracles, it would have been easier to follow Him"? How does Jesus' statement in verse 7 address this type of thinking?

What does Jesus say that the Helper will do with regard to "the world"?

Do you think this involves believers? Why/why not?

According to verse 12, has Jesus spoken everything the disciples need to hear? Why/why not?

What does this tell you about Jesus? Does this encourage you? If so, how specifically?

Now, let's take a quick step back and remember who is speaking to whom here. According to the context, who is the "you" of verse 13?

What will the Helper, the Spirit of truth, do for them when He comes?

What will He disclose? To whom? From whom?

What are some ways the Spirit guided the disciples and the early Church into all the truth?

Who does the Spirit bring glory to? Why does this matter?

@THE END OF THE DAY . . .

Take some time to talk to God about what you learned this week. Then, write down your most significant application point. How will you apply this today?

LESSON SIX: **An Unexpected Advantage!**

From Grief to Joy!

". . . you will grieve, but your grief will be turned into joy."
—Jesus, John 16:20b

No one wants sorrow and no one seeks out grief but both are part of the fallen sinful condition. Each is common to man. Jesus, who became a man and took on flesh and blood, understands. When sorrow fills the disciples' hearts, Jesus sees it and *understands,* knowing firsthand the emotions His beloved disciples are experiencing and will face in the coming days.

He doesn't brush off their concerns as unimportant. Rather He frames them in light of the bigger picture, setting the ephemeral, the transitory, against the eternal. They will face real grief, and tribulation will be a constant reality *in this world,* but even in the midst of storms He is near!

Like tarnish polished off silver, grief for the believer eventually gives way to joy!

Are you remembering to pray?

As we're studying and learning more about the Holy Spirit, remember to keep praying and asking that He will help you learn and apply God's Word.

JOY
FROM THE
UPPER ROOM
John 13-17

LESSON SEVEN: **From Grief to Joy!**

REMEMBERING

As a way of locking truth into your long-term memory and hiding the principles in your heart, let's be a little more specific this week in our review. Think through John 13–15 chapter-by-chapter and then segment-by-segment. Give each chapter a #hashtag and include as many segments (with verse ranges) and #hashtags within each chapter as are helpful to you.

John 13 # _____

John 14 #_____

John 15 # _____

How are you doing with the business of loving one another?

How are you doing at showing love specifically to those who are *difficult* for you to love? (Sorry, had to ask.)

OVERVIEW JOHN 16

Yes, let's read the whole chapter to keep ourselves in context.

OBSERVE the TEXT of SCRIPTURE

READ John 16 and **MARK** any key words you identify.

John 16

1   *"These things I have spoken to you so that you may be kept from stumbling.*

2   *"They will make you outcasts from the synagogue, but an hour is coming for everyone who kills you to think that he is offering service to God.*

3   *"These things they will do because they have not known the Father or Me.*

4   *"But these things I have spoken to you, so that when their hour comes, you may remember that I told you of them. These things I did not say to you at the beginning, because I was with you.*

5   *"But now I am going to Him who sent Me; and none of you asks Me, 'Where are You going?'*

6   *"But because I have said these things to you, sorrow has filled your heart.*

7   *"But I tell you the truth, it is to your advantage that I go away; for if I do not go away, the Helper will not come to you; but if I go, I will send Him to you.*

8   *"And He, when He comes, will convict the world concerning sin and righteousness and judgment;*

9   *concerning sin, because they do not believe in Me;*

10 *and concerning righteousness, because I go to the Father and you no longer see Me;*

11 *and concerning judgment, because the ruler of this world has been judged.*

12 *"I have many more things to say to you, but you cannot bear them now.*

13 *"But when He, the Spirit of truth, comes, He will guide you into all the truth; for He will not speak on His own initiative, but whatever He hears, He will speak; and He will disclose to you what is to come.*

14 *"He will glorify Me, for He will take of Mine and will disclose it to you.*

15 *"All things that the Father has are Mine; therefore I said that He takes of Mine and will disclose it to you.*

16 *"A little while, and you will no longer see Me; and again a little while, and you will see Me."*

17 *Some of His disciples then said to one another, "What is this thing He is telling us, 'A little while, and you will not see Me; and again a little while, and you will see Me'; and, 'because I go to the Father'?"*

18 *So they were saying, "What is this that He says, 'A little while'? We do not know what He is talking about."*

19 *Jesus knew that they wished to question Him, and He said to them, "Are you deliberating together about this, that I said, 'A little while, and you will not see Me, and again a little while, and you will see Me'?*

JOY
FROM THE
UPPER ROOM
John 13-17

LESSON SEVEN: **From Grief to Joy!**

20 *"Truly, truly, I say to you, that you will weep and lament, but the world will rejoice; you will grieve, but your grief will be turned into joy.*

21 *"Whenever a woman is in labor she has pain, because her hour has come; but when she gives birth to the child, she no longer remembers the anguish because of the joy that a child has been born into the world.*

22 *"Therefore you too have grief now; but I will see you again, and your heart will rejoice, and no one will take your joy away from you.*

23 *"In that day you will not question Me about anything. Truly, truly, I say to you, if you ask the Father for anything in My name, He will give it to you.*

24 *"Until now you have asked for nothing in My name; ask and you will receive, so that your joy may be made full.*

25 *"These things I have spoken to you in figurative language; an hour is coming when I will no longer speak to you in figurative language, but will tell you plainly of the Father.*

26 *"In that day you will ask in My name, and I do not say to you that I will request of the Father on your behalf;*

27 *for the Father Himself loves you, because you have loved Me and have believed that I came forth from the Father.*

28 *"I came forth from the Father and have come into the world; I am leaving the world again and going to the Father."*

29 *His disciples said, "Lo, now You are speaking plainly and are not using a figure of speech.*

30 *"Now we know that You know all things, and have no need for anyone to question You; by this we believe that You came from God."*

31 *Jesus answered them, "Do you now believe?*

32 *"Behold, an hour is coming, and has already come, for you to be scattered, each to his own home, and to leave Me alone; and yet I am not alone, because the Father is with Me.*

33 *"These things I have spoken to you, so that in Me you may have peace. In the world you have tribulation, but take courage; I have overcome the world."*

DISCUSS with your GROUP or PONDER on your own . . .

Write down anything of interest that you noticed for the first time on this read-through.

What questions do you still have that you'd like to find answers to in the Word?

LOOKING CLOSER . . .

As we look at this section of the text, time phrases will be a key element to watch.

OBSERVE the TEXT of SCRIPTURE

READ John 16:16-22 and **MARK** the phrase *a little while*, as well as the words *grief* and *joy*.

John 16:16-22

16 *"A little while, and you will no longer see Me; and again a little while, and you will see Me."*

17 *Some of His disciples then said to one another, "What is this thing He is telling us, 'A little while, and you will not see Me; and again a little while, and you will see Me'; and, 'because I go to the Father'?"*

18 *So they were saying, "What is this that He says, 'A little while'? We do not know what He is talking about."*

19 *Jesus knew that they wished to question Him, and He said to them, "Are you deliberating together about this, that I said, 'A little while, and you will not see Me, and again a little while, and you will see Me'?*

20 *"Truly, truly, I say to you, that you will weep and lament, but the world will rejoice; you will grieve, but your grief will be turned into joy.*

21 *"Whenever a woman is in labor she has pain, because her hour has come; but when she gives birth to the child, she no longer remembers the anguish because of the joy that a child has been born into the world.*

22 *"Therefore you too have grief now; but I will see you again, and your heart will rejoice, and no one will take your joy away from you."*

DISCUSS with your GROUP or PONDER on your own . . .

What does Jesus say is going to happen "in a little while"?

How do His disciples respond to His statement? What confuses them?

LESSON SEVEN: **From Grief to Joy!**

Let's examine how the phrase "a little while" has been used before in John. (The verses are in the FYI box to the left.)

John 7:33

John 12:35

John 13:33

John 14:19

At this point, what do you think Jesus' "a little while" refers to? Why?

Do the disciples ever get around to asking Jesus about their question? What happens instead?

What does Jesus tell them about coming events? How will the world respond? How will the disciples feel?

What comparison does Jesus make in verse 21?

FYI:

For Your Convenience
I've made the phrase **"a little while"** boldface in the following verses so it's easier to compare.

John 7:33
*Therefore Jesus said, "For **a little while** longer I am with you, then I go to Him who sent Me."*

John 12:35
*So Jesus said to them, "For **a little while** longer the Light is among you. Walk while you have the Light, so that darkness will not overtake you; he who walks in the darkness does not know where he goes."*

John 13:33
*"Little children, I am with you **a little while** longer. You will seek Me; and as I said to the Jews, now I also say to you, 'Where I am going, you cannot come.'"*

John 14:19
*"After **a little while** the world will no longer see Me, but you will see Me; because I live, you will live also."*

How will the disciples' situation change?

Before we move on, list specifically the "negative" or "hard" things that they will do or experience.

How does Jesus encourage them? What will bring permanent joy?

Is there something you are grieving, weeping over, or lamenting today? What has caused the pain?

Does Jesus tell His disciples to run away from grief? Does He condemn their feelings of grief as wrong in any way? Explain.

If you are in a place of grief today, write a brief prayer to God telling Him about your pain and asking Him to help you see the joy He has for you.

FYI:

A Dot on the Line of Eternity

Perspective. You and I naturally have a human perspective because we live within time. Today follows yesterday and precedes tomorrow. When affliction and hardship come, our natural inclination is to push back or run away to make the here-and-now feel better and more tolerable. God's people, though, are to have another perspective, a different perspective that measures time not man's way but God's way and prioritizes long-term outcomes over short-term comfort.

Listen to God's Word through the Apostle Paul in 2 Corinthians 4:16-18:

"Therefore we do not lose heart, but though our outer man is decaying, yet our inner man is being renewed day by day. For momentary, light affliction is producing for us an eternal weight of glory far beyond all comparison, while we look not at the things which are seen, but at the things which are not seen; for the things which are seen are temporal, but the things which are not seen are eternal."

This moment is not all that is. This moment, as has often been said, is but a dot on the line of eternity.

JOY

LESSON SEVEN: **From Grief to Joy!**

Digging Deeper

What Does the Bible Say About Suffering and Affliction

How often do our prayers focus on relieving suffering for ourselves or those we love? But what if God uses affliction in our lives?

Take some time this week to discover what the Bible teaches about suffering. What, if anything, causes suffering? Does it yield any benefit? Is it something to be avoided at all cost? Go ahead and explore this topic on your own using a concordance and your Bible.

If you need some help getting started, here are a few suggestions to spur you along: Isaiah 53, Job, Romans 5, 2 Corinthians 4, James 1.

OBSERVE the TEXT of SCRIPTURE

READ John 16:23-33 and **MARK** distinctively the phrase *"ask in My name"* and the words *question/request.* Also **MARK** any references to time that you notice.

John 16:23-33

23 *"In that day you will not question Me about anything. Truly, truly, I say to you, if you ask the Father for anything in My name, He will give it to you.*

24 *"Until now you have asked for nothing in My name; ask and you will receive, so that your joy may be made full.*

25 *"These things I have spoken to you in figurative language; an hour is coming when I will no longer speak to you in figurative language, but will tell you plainly of the Father.*

26 *"In that day you will ask in My name, and I do not say to you that I will request of the Father on your behalf;*

27 *for the Father Himself loves you, because you have loved Me and have believed that I came forth from the Father.*

28 *"I came forth from the Father and have come into the world; I am leaving the world again and going to the Father."*

29 *His disciples said, "Lo, now You are speaking plainly and are not using a figure of speech.*

30 *"Now we know that You know all things, and have no need for anyone to question You; by this we believe that You came from God."*

31 *Jesus answered them, "Do you now believe?*

32 *"Behold, an hour is coming, and has already come, for you to be scattered, each to his own home, and to leave Me alone; and yet I am not alone, because the Father is with Me.*

33 *"These things I have spoken to you, so that in Me you may have peace. In the world you have tribulation, but take courage; I have overcome the world."*

ONE STEP FURTHER:

When the Disciples Asked

If you have some time this week, check out Mark 10:35-45 to see what can happen when we try to make Jesus follow our orders! Record your observations below and evaluate your own prayer life. How often do you make similar requests? What, if anything, needs to change in your prayer life?

DISCUSS with your GROUP or PONDER on your own . . .

Thinking back to the last section of the text (verse 19), what had the disciples wanted to do (but didn't)?

What does Jesus say about the content of their prayers changing?

JOY
FROM THE
UPPER ROOM
John 13-17

ONE STEP FURTHER:

Asking in Jesus' Name

You may already have looked at this in a previous **Digging Deeper** section. If you haven't, though, take some time to explore what it means to ask something in Jesus' name.

Here are a few chapters to peruse:

Acts 3

Acts 4

Acts 9

Philippians 2

Summarize what you learned about asking in Jesus' name:

LESSON SEVEN: **From Grief to Joy!**

Let's look at this by making two simple lists. Record what has been happening (what the disciples have/haven't asked for; how Jesus has been speaking to them, etc.) and what they will do "in that day."

Until now . . .   **In that day . . .**

What statement causes the disciples to say Jesus is finally "speaking plainly"? What do they declare based on this statement?

How does Jesus respond to their declaration? What does He tell them is about to happen to them and to Him?

According to verse 33, why did Jesus say "these things" to the disciples?

Now, let's take some time to think through what we've observed in the text. Some of these questions may sound like review, but I want us to reason through the text together.

What promise does Jesus make in verse 23?

What will "asking and receiving" from God bring the disciples?

Digging Deeper

What Kind of Prayers Does God Answer?

If you have time this week, see what you can discover about prayer. As a first step, you'll want to use a concordance to find where prayer is mentioned throughout the Bible and what is said about it. (As you search, note the original-language words you find and search again using the Greek and Hebrew as your search terms to see if you can find additional results.)

You've probably already realized that searching on "pray" and "prayer" will give you much information but not all of it. What other synonyms might tell you more about prayer? Search on those, too. Then record what you learn.

Summarize what you learned about prayer. Does this encourage you about your current prayer life? Does it spur you towards biblical change? Explain.

JOY
FROM THE
UPPER ROOM
John 13-17

LESSON SEVEN: **From Grief to Joy!**

What problem does thinking our prayers are not being answered bring up?

Have you ever felt like your prayers were not being answered? How has that affected you? What have you done with that feeling?

Let's go back to the text. Is Jesus' promise in verse 23 in any way limited? If so, how?

Let's look at two near-context verses (included in the FYI box to the left) that relate to Jesus' "name." How is the reference to Jesus' name used in each? How might each of these help us to understand what it means to pray in Jesus' name?

John 14:26

John 15:21

What in the texts point to other limits? Since Jesus tells His disciples that they *will* have tribulation in the world, do you think it's logical for them to think they *can* pray it away? Explain.

FYI:

For Your Convenience
Again, I've boldfaced the phrase we're looking at.

John 14:26
*"But the Helper, the Holy Spirit, whom the Father will send **in My name,** He will teach you all things, and bring to your remembrance all that I said to you."*

John 15:21
*"But all these things they will do to you **for My name's sake,** because they do not know the One who sent Me."*

If a friend of yours were to do something "in your name," what would you expect of them? How would you expect it to compare with your person and beliefs?

What do we as a people typically pray for? What do you pray for? How does this compare with what Jesus prays for?

Do you know the kinds of things that Jesus wants you pray for? If so, what are some of them? If not, how can you find this out?

Where in your life do you need peace? How can "these things" Jesus spoke remind you of the peace believers have in Him?

What are ways you can "take courage" today because of Jesus' victory?

@THE END OF THE DAY . . .

Remember, while tribulation is part of the story, for believers it is not the end of the story! Jesus has overcome the world—so take courage, live in the peace He provides, and embrace the fullness of joy He has for you!

ONE STEP FURTHER:

Word Study: *Take Courage*

If you have some time this week, see what you can find out about the Greek verb translated "take courage." Record your findings below.

JOY
FROM THE
UPPER ROOM
John 13-17

LESSON SEVEN: **From Grief to Joy!**

Jesus Prays for You!

"I do not ask on behalf of these alone,
but for those also who believe in Me through their word . . . ."
—Jesus, John 17:20

In reading the Bible, we pick up over its pages that Jesus and the Spirit intercede for believers to the Father. In 1 Timothy 2:5-6, Paul says "For there is one God, *and* one mediator also between God and men, *the* man Jesus Christ, who gave Himself a ransom for all, the testimony *given* at the proper time." Based on this intercessory work of Jesus, Paul calls men everywhere to pray.

In Romans, Paul speaks of the work of the Spirit in prayer saying, "In the same way the Spirit also helps our weakness; for we do not know how to pray as we should, but the Spirit Himself intercedes for *us* with groanings too deep for words; and He who searches the hearts knows what the mind of the Spirit is because He intercedes for the saints according to *the will of* God" (Romans 8:26-27).

As believers we are exhorted to pray without ceasing (1 Thessalonians 5:17), but we are not called to this work alone. We see throughout the New Testament the working of the Son and the Holy Spirit on behalf of believers, but in John 17 we get a glimpse into the prayer life of Jesus as He prays for His disciples then and now!

 FYI:

You've Made It!!

Here you are! You've made it to Lesson 8! You're either feeling super-accomplished because you've finished strong or, maybe, you're limping across the finish line and haven't even put pencil to paper in the past several weeks. Whichever it is, tomorrow is the next day of seeking after God. If you're moving into a season without a regular Bible study, what is your plan for maintaining a regular time with God? Do you have accountability built into your life? If not, why not consider reaching out to another branch or a group of branches so you can encourage and be encouraged to abide in the true Vine.

REMEMBERING

Take a few minutes to jot down what you've learned so far, focusing primarily on how God has been using John 13–17 to change how you think and act.

Before we move on, how would a close friend or family member say this study has been changing you? If the main change has been in your thinking, don't make something up—just move along to the next section.

OVERVIEW JOHN 17

Let's look at the final chapter in our study—John 17!

OBSERVE the TEXT of SCRIPTURE

READ John 17 and **MARK** references to *Jesus* and *the Father*.

John 17

1 *Jesus spoke these things; and lifting up His eyes to heaven, He said, "Father, the hour has come; glorify Your Son, that the Son may glorify You,*

2 *even as You gave Him authority over all flesh, that to all whom You have given Him, He may give eternal life.*

3 *"This is eternal life, that they may know You, the only true God, and Jesus Christ whom You have sent.*

4 *"I glorified You on the earth, having accomplished the work which You have given Me to do.*

5 *"Now, Father, glorify Me together with Yourself, with the glory which I had with You before the world was.*

6 *"I have manifested Your name to the men whom You gave Me out of the world; they were Yours and You gave them to Me, and they have kept Your word.*

7 *"Now they have come to know that everything You have given Me is from You;*

ONE STEP FURTHER:

Some Verse Suggestions by Chapter

In the best of all possible worlds, we'd all have memorized John 13–17. Alas, you and I live in a broken and fallen world. If you thought about memorizing but never got around to it, may I suggest a representative verse from each of our chapters of study to memorize? You know, just in case you find yourself bored when this class ends!

John 13:14—Foot Washing

"If I then, the Lord and the Teacher, washed your feet, you also ought to wash one another's feet."

John 14:6—One Way

"Jesus said to him, 'I am the way, and the truth, and the life; no one comes to the Father but through Me'."

John 15:4, 12—Abide and Love

"Abide in Me, and I in you. As the branch cannot bear fruit of itself unless it abides in the vine, so neither can you unless you abide in Me."

"This is My commandment, that you love one another, just as I have loved you."

John 16:7—The Helper

"But I tell you the truth, it is to your advantage that I go away; for if I do not go away, the Helper will not come to you; but if I go, I will send Him to you."

John 17:17—Jesus' Prayer

"Sanctify them in the truth; Your word is truth."

8 *for the words which You gave Me I have given to them; and they received them and truly understood that I came forth from You, and they believed that You sent Me.*

9 *"I ask on their behalf; I do not ask on behalf of the world, but of those whom You have given Me; for they are Yours;*

10 *and all things that are Mine are Yours, and Yours are Mine; and I have been glorified in them.*

11 *"I am no longer in the world; and yet they themselves are in the world, and I come to You. Holy Father, keep them in Your name, the name which You have given Me, that they may be one even as We are.*

12 *"While I was with them, I was keeping them in Your name which You have given Me; and I guarded them and not one of them perished but the son of perdition, so that the Scripture would be fulfilled.*

13 *"But now I come to You; and these things I speak in the world so that they may have My joy made full in themselves.*

14 *"I have given them Your word; and the world has hated them, because they are not of the world, even as I am not of the world.*

15 *"I do not ask You to take them out of the world, but to keep them from the evil one.*

16 *"They are not of the world, even as I am not of the world.*

17 *"Sanctify them in the truth; Your word is truth.*

18 *"As You sent Me into the world, I also have sent them into the world.*

19 *"For their sakes I sanctify Myself, that they themselves also may be sanctified in truth.*

20 *"I do not ask on behalf of these alone, but for those also who believe in Me through their word;*

21 *that they may all be one; even as You, Father, are in Me and I in You, that they also may be in Us, so that the world may believe that You sent Me.*

22 *"The glory which You have given Me I have given to them, that they may be one, just as We are one;*

23 *I in them and You in Me, that they may be perfected in unity, so that the world may know that You sent Me, and loved them, even as You have loved Me.*

24 *"Father, I desire that they also, whom You have given Me, be with Me where I am, so that they may see My glory which You have given Me, for You loved Me before the foundation of the world.*

25 *"O righteous Father, although the world has not known You, yet I have known You; and these have known that You sent Me;*

26 *and I have made Your name known to them, and will make it known, so that the love with which You loved Me may be in them, and I in them."*

JOY
FROM THE
UPPER ROOM
John 13-17

LESSON EIGHT: **Jesus Prays for You!**

DISCUSS with your GROUP or PONDER on your own . . .

What are your general observations on John 17?

What did you learn about the Son?

The Father?

What questions do you want answered?

LOOKING CLOSER . . .

Let's slow down and look more closely at Jesus' prayer to the Father.

OBSERVE the TEXT of SCRIPTURE

READ John 17:1-5 and **MARK** in a distinctive way, references to *glory/glorify/glorified; gave/given;* and *eternal life.*

John 17:1-5

1 *Jesus spoke these things; and lifting up His eyes to heaven, He said, "Father, the hour has come; glorify Your Son, that the Son may glorify You,*

2 *even as You gave Him authority over all flesh, that to all whom You have given Him, He may give eternal life.*

3 *"This is eternal life, that they may know You, the only true God, and Jesus Christ whom You have sent.*

4 *"I glorified You on the earth, having accomplished the work which You have given Me to do.*

5 *"Now, Father, glorify Me together with Yourself, with the glory which I had with You before the world was."*

FYI:

Kavod
The Hebrew word translated "glory" is *kavod*. Its root has the basic meaning of "heavy" or "weighty."

DISCUSS with your GROUP or PONDER on your own . . .

What major shift happens between John 16 and John 17? Who is Jesus now talking to?

What time phrase did you notice in verse 1? What is this referring to?

What is the first request Jesus makes the Father?

List what you learned by marking "glory/glorify/glorified."

JOY
FROM THE
UPPER ROOM
John 13-17

FYI:

"Glorified" Cross-References

Here are some near-context cross-references on **glorified.**

John 14:13

*"Whatever you ask in My name, that will I do, so that the Father may be **glorified** in the Son."*

John 15:8

*"My Father is **glorified** by this, that you bear much fruit, and so prove to be My disciples."*

LESSON EIGHT: **Jesus Prays for You!**

What has Jesus already said about ways His disciples glorify the Father? (See John 14:13, John 15:8 in the sidebar.)

How does Jesus glorify the Father on earth? What does it eventually entail?

What do we learn about Jesus' pre-existence in this passage?

What had the Father given to Jesus? How does Jesus respond?

How does Jesus define eternal life? Do you have eternal life? If so, how do you know?

Does Jesus' definition make evangelism seem less intimidating? Explain your thoughts.

Digging Deeper

The Good News About Jesus

The entire Bible teaches the Gospel of Jesus Christ—the good news of how God reconciled man to Himself in Christ. I'm going to give you some basic verses (that you are probably familiar with!) that lay the groundwork for the bad news and the good news of the gospel. What other biblical texts can you use to explain the good news of Jesus to others?

The Bad News
Romans 3:23

Romans 6:23

The Good News
Romans 5:8

Ephesians 2:8-9

My favorites for sharing Jesus . . .

ONE STEP FURTHER:

In the Beginning . . .
Before the world was, Jesus already existed. If you have some time this week, examine the first chapter of Genesis and compare it with the first chapter of John. Note the similarities and consider whether John can help us interpret the use of the plural pronouns in Genesis 1:26. Record your findings below.

LESSON EIGHT: **Jesus Prays for You!**

Digging Deeper

Eternal Life

As you explore the Bible to find out what it says about eternal life, you'll need to think in terms of synonyms as you hunt. Clearly you can start your search on the word "eternal," but you'll need to think of other words or phrases with the same or similar meanings, for instance, "everlasting" or "will not die." Or you can start with a more general search on "life" and sift your way through concordance entries.

As you do, realize that there are different ways to go about this assignment, so don't get stressed out over whether or not you're doing it "right." After all, the available tools change almost daily, so there will always be a new and improved way to search—that's a good thing!

Old Testament View of Life and Death

Jesus' Words on Eternal Life

How Paul Explains Eternal Life in Christ

How Other New Testament Writers Explain Eternal Life

My summary . . .

OBSERVE the TEXT of SCRIPTURE

READ John 17:6-12 and **MARK** every reference to the disciples. The first reference is *the men whom You gave Me out of the world*. Let's also **MARK** *keep/kept/keeping* and *guarded*. Finally, **MARK** references to *the world*.

John 17:6-12

6 *"I have manifested Your name to the men whom You gave Me out of the world; they were Yours and You gave them to Me, and they have kept Your word.*

7 *"Now they have come to know that everything You have given Me is from You;*

8 *for the words which You gave Me I have given to them; and they received them and truly understood that I came forth from You, and they believed that You sent Me.*

9 *"I ask on their behalf; I do not ask on behalf of the world, but of those whom You have given Me; for they are Yours;*

10 *and all things that are Mine are Yours, and Yours are Mine; and I have been glorified in them.*

11 *"I am no longer in the world; and yet they themselves are in the world, and I come to You. Holy Father, keep them in Your name, the name which You have given Me, that they may be one even as We are.*

12 *"While I was with them, I was keeping them in Your name which You have given Me; and I guarded them and not one of them perished but the son of perdition, so that the Scripture would be fulfilled."*

FYI:

What about Judas?
Although the "son of perdition" perished, none of those *given to* Jesus did. The only other occurrence of the phrase "son of perdition/destruction" (Greek: *huios tes apoleias*) is in 2 Thessalonians 2:3 where Paul uses it to describe the anti-Christ. Judas, to be sure, was not *the* anti-Christ, but in opposing and betraying Christ displayed anti-Christ characteristics.

DISCUSS with your GROUP or PONDER on your own . . .

What is the focus of Jesus' prayer in this section?

List what you learned about "the men" Jesus prays for.

Who do these men belong to? Why?

JOY
FROM THE
UPPER ROOM
John 13-17

LESSON EIGHT: **Jesus Prays for You!**

What have they come to know and how have they come to know it?

How does Jesus pray for them specifically?

What does Jesus say about the world?

What does Jesus say about the Father's name in verses 11-12? How does it relate to His name?

According to verse 11, why does Jesus want His disciples to be kept in the Father's name? What benefit is there?

Does knowing that God guards His people give you confidence? What specific fears can that help combat in your life?

OBSERVE the TEXT of SCRIPTURE

READ John 17:13-21 and **MARK** references to the *word* and *truth*. Continue to **MARK** references to *the world.*

John 17:13-21

13 "But now I come to You; and these things I speak in the world so that they may have My joy made full in themselves.

14 "I have given them Your word; and the world has hated them, because they are not of the world, even as I am not of the world.

15 "I do not ask You to take them out of the world, but to keep them from the evil one.

16 "They are not of the world, even as I am not of the world.

17 "Sanctify them in the truth; Your word is truth.

18 "As You sent Me into the world, I also have sent them into the world.

19 "For their sakes I sanctify Myself, that they themselves also may be sanctified in truth.

20 "I do not ask on behalf of these alone, but for those also who believe in Me through their word;

21 that they may all be one; even as You, Father, are in Me and I in You, that they also may be in Us, so that the world may believe that You sent Me."

DISCUSS with your GROUP or PONDER on your own . . .

Why does Jesus say He is speaking these things now?

How does He describe the joy He refers to? Whose joy is it and where will it be?

How will the disciples be able to live in and experience this joy? What has Jesus told them about it? How does it relate to what He has been talking about?

JOY
FROM THE
UPPER ROOM
John 13-17

ONE STEP FURTHER:

Word Study: *Sanctify*

Take some time this week to look into the verb "sanctify." Find the Greek root and then see where else and how else it is used in John and the rest of the New Testament. Then answer these question: *Why does Jesus need to "sanctify Himself" and how does that relate to us? Does the Bible say anything else about Jesus being sanctified?* Record your findings below.

LESSON EIGHT: **Jesus Prays for You!**

According to verse 14, what has Jesus given to His disciples? What does He say God's Word is?

What reaction does the world have to Jesus' followers? Why?

Do you ever find yourself struggling for acceptance by the world? If so, how?

What is the believer's purpose in the world? Explain.

What, then, should your relationship with the world be? Think in practical, everyday scenarios. Should Christians be living entirely separate lives from the world . . . or not? Support your view from Scripture.

What does Jesus pray for in verses 15, 16, and 21? What difference will this make in the life of a believer? In your life?

JOY
FROM THE
UPPER ROOM
John 13-17

According to verse 20, who is He praying for in these verses?!

Have you ever wanted to know God's Word better? John 17:17 is a prayer you can pray for yourself, knowing that it is Jesus' will because He has already prayed it! You may want to write down a prayer to that effect right now. Hey, there's space below!

What does unity in the Body testify to the world? What will be the unifying factor?

So, put another way, what is one of the major goals of you and I loving both God *and* one another?

How can you be a part of fostering true unity in your church? How do you think this might affect the greater community?

Before we move on, is there anything in your life that you need to repent of? Are you holding on to any anger or grudges against others in the Body that are a barrier to unity? If so, why not write them down, *set* them down, and ask God to forgive you and heal your heart.

JOY
FROM THE
UPPER ROOM
John 13–17

LESSON EIGHT: **Jesus Prays for You!**

OBSERVE the TEXT of SCRIPTURE

READ John 17:22-26 and **MARK** occurrences of *love(d)* and *known*.

John 17:22-26

22 *"The glory which You have given Me I have given to them, that they may be one, just as We are one;*

23 *I in them and You in Me, that they may be perfected in unity, so that the world may know that You sent Me, and loved them, even as You have loved Me.*

24 *"Father, I desire that they also, whom You have given Me, be with Me where I am, so that they may see My glory which You have given Me, for You loved Me before the foundation of the world.*

25 *"O righteous Father, although the world has not known You, yet I have known You; and these have known that You sent Me;*

26 *and I have made Your name known to them, and will make it known, so that the love with which You loved Me may be in them, and I in them."*

DISCUSS with your GROUP or PONDER on your own . . .

What does Jesus say He has given to His disciples and for what purpose?

As best you can, illustrate the relationship Jesus describes in verse 23.

When believers are perfected in unity what will this help the world to know about Jesus? About believers?

What does Jesus desire and pray for in verse 24? Do you desire the same or are your more pressing desires here on earth? Just asking.

FYI:

Complete
When Jesus asks that we be "perfected" in unity, the Greek verb used is *teleioo* which means "to complete."

What do we learn about the timing of the relationship between the Father and the Son?

What do believers know that the world does not? How do they know it?

Looking back over the pages of John 13–17, what attitudes will characterize Jesus' followers even after He leaves and why?

Are these becoming more a part of your life day by day? If so, where do you see growth? What areas are harder?

@THE END OF THE DAY . . .

As we come to the close of our time together, here are some application questions to keep in mind and think on in the days ahead.

What are some specific ways you can "love one another" in your local church?

How can you demonstrate Christ's love to your unbelieving friends and family?

LESSON EIGHT: **Jesus Prays for You!**

What threatens to drain your joy in the coming days and weeks? How can you choose joy instead based on John 13–17?

How do you plan to abide in the Vine tomorrow? Next month? Next year?

"I am the vine,
you are the branches;
he who abides in Me and I in him,
he bears much fruit,
for apart from Me you can do nothing."

—Jesus, John 15:5

Biblical joy is a contentment of the soul grounded in the finished work of Jesus that cannot be taken away. Sometimes, though, we feel that it is waning. When that happens, ask yourself these five questions:

1. Am I abiding in the True Vine? Just as branches draw life from the vine, our joy flourishes when we remain connected to Jesus—the source of all joy.

2. Am I "one-anothering"? Walking with others who are walking with Jesus fosters joy in us.

3. Am I remembering the finished work of Jesus? Joy is ultimately grounded in what Jesus did for us. He conquered sin and death to restore us to a right relationship with the Father. Remembering and relying on that truth will bring joy.

4. Am I praying on-mission prayers? Our joy deepens when we align our prayers with God's heart. Praying in accordance with His will and His mission, and seeing those answered, will bring us joy.

5. Am I walking by the Spirit or am I quenching His work in my life? Am I listening and responding? Surrender to the Spirit's leading brings joy.

It is my prayer that we will each take the truths we've learned in John 13-17 and apply them in our lives so that His joy will overflow in our hearts. May we walk in His grace, His truth, His peace, His love, and in His joy!

RESOURCES

Helpful Study Tools

How to Study Your Bible
Eugene, Oregon: Harvest House
Publishers

The New Inductive Study Bible
Eugene, Oregon: Harvest House
Publishers

Logos Bible Software
Available at www.logos.com.

Greek Word Study Tools

Kittel, G., Friedrich, G., & Bromiley,
G.W.
*Theological Dictionary of the New
Testament, Abridged* (also known as
Little Kittel)
Grand Rapids, Michigan: W.B.
Eerdmans Publishing Company

Hebrew Word Study Tools

Harris, R.L., Archer, G.L., & Walker,
B.K.
*Theological Wordbook of the Old
Testament* (also known as TWOT)
Chicago, Illinois: Moody Press

General Word Study Tools

Strong, James
*The New Strong's Exhaustive
Concordance of the Bible*
Nashville, Tennessee: Thomas Nelson

Recommended Commentary Sets

Expositor's Bible Commentary
Grand Rapids, Michigan: Zondervan

NIV Application Commentary
Grand Rapids, Michigan: Zondervan

The New American Commentary
Nashville, Tennessee: Broadman and
Holman Publishers

One-Volume Commentary

Carson, D.A., France, R.T., Motyer,
J.A., & Wenham, G.J. Ed.
*New Bible Commentary: 21st Century
Edition*
Downers Grove, Illinois: Inter-Varsity
Press

Rydelnik, M.,.Vanlaningham, M., Ed.
The Moody Bible Commentary
Chicago, Illinois: Moody Publishers

HOW TO DO AN ONLINE WORD STUDY

For use with www.blueletterbible.org

1. Type in Bible verse. Change the version to NASB. Click the "Search" button.

2. When you arrive at the next screen, you will see a "Tools" button to the left of your verse .

3. Hover over the "Tools" button and select the "Interlinear" option to take you to the concordance link.

3. Click on the Strong's number which is the link to the original word in Greek or Hebrew.

Clicking this number will bring up another screen that will give you a brief definition of the word as well as list every occurrence of the Greek word in the New Testament or Hebrew word in the Old Testament. Before running to the dictionary definition, scan places where this word is used in Scripture and examine the general contexts where it is used.

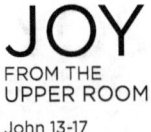

Learn more

Find more books, studies, and resources at

www.pamgillaspie.com

Connect with others

Be an ambassador. FOLLOW, LOVE, and SHARE us on social media.

 pamgillaspie

 pamgillaspie